Merry Christmas 2009, to my
very special friend Sa
Always Thinking o
Sandie

In Praise of
Labs

With stories by James Herriot, Gary Paulsen, Gene Hill, Bill Tarrant,
Roger Welsch, Ted Kerasote, Kenny Salwey, Ron Schara, and more
Photographs by Lynn M. Stone

Voyageur Press

First published in 2007 by MBI Publishing Company LLC and Voyageur Press, an imprint of MBI Publishing Company LLC, Galtier Plaza, Suite 200, 380 Jackson Street, St. Paul, MN 55101 USA

The information in this book is true and complete to the best of our knowledge. All recommendations are made without any guarantee on the part of the author or Publisher, who also disclaim any liability incurred in connection with the use of this data or specific details.

We recognize, further, that some words, model names, and designations mentioned herein are the property of the trademark holder. We use them for identification purposes only. This is not an official publication.

Voyageur Press titles are also available at discounts in bulk quantity for industrial or sales-promotional use. For details write to Special Sales Manager at MBI Publishing Company, Galtier Plaza, Suite 200, 380 Jackson Street, St. Paul, MN 55101 USA.

To find out more about our books, join us online at www.voyageurpress.com.

Library of Congress Cataloging-in-Publication Data

In praise of labs : celebrating the world's greatest dog with stories /
by James Herriot ...[et al.] ; photography by Lynn M. Stone.
    p. cm.
  ISBN-13: 978-0-7603-2813-2 (plc w/ jacket)
  1. Labrador retriever--Anecdotes. 2. Labrador retriever--Pictorial
works. I. Herriot, James. II. Stone, Lynn M.
SF429.L3154 2007
636.752'7--dc22
                            2007020328

Designer: Chris Fayers

Printed in China

Permissions
We have made every effort to determine original sources and locate copyright holders of the excerpts in this book. Grateful acknowledgment is made to the writers, publishers, and agencies listed below for permission to reprint material copyrighted or controlled by them. Please bring to our attention any errors of fact, omission, or copyright.
    "It's A Dog's Life" by Gene Hill. Copyright © 1993 by Gene Hill. Reprinted by permission of the author.
"The Bonded, or Imprinted, Dog" by Bill Tarrant. Copyright © 1999 by Bill Tarrant. Reprinted by permission of the author's estate.
    "The Dustbin Dog" from *The Lord God Made Them All* by James Herriot. Copyright © 1981 by James Herriot. Reprinted by permission of St. Martin's Press Inc. Reprinted in the United Kingdom and Commonwealth by permission of David Higham Associates for Michael Joseph Limited.
    "From the Wild" from *Merle's Door: Lessons from a Freethinking Dog* by Ted Kerasote. Copyright © 2007 by Ted Kerasote. Reprinted by permission of Harcourt.
    "What's in a Name" from *A Life With Dogs* by Roger Welsch. Copyright © 2004 by Roger Welsch. Reprinted by permission of the author.
    "Ike: A Good Friend" from *My Life in Dog Years* by Gary Paulsen. Copyright © 1998 by Gary Paulsen. Reprinted by permission of Flannery Literary.
    "A Man and His Dog" by Ron Schara. Copyright © 1993 by Ron Schara. Reprinted by permission of the author.
    "Old Spook and the Last Duck Hunt" from *The Last River Rat: Kenny Salwey's Life in the Wild* by Kenny Salwey. Copyright © 2001 by Kenny Salwey. Reprinted by permission of the author.

Photographs on pages 36–39 and 58–59 are courtesy of Shutterstock.

Contents

Introduction

In Praise of Labs

For those of us with Labrador retrievers in our lives, it's often difficult to remember a time when we were not surrounded by Labs. These dogs have a grip on us, a hold on our very being.

It should be little surprise that Labrador retrievers are the most popular dog in North America. Labs surpassed cocker spaniels in the 1960s as our favorites, according to the American Kennel Club's annual registrations. Golden retrievers are a distant second, and spaniels remain popular. But Labs have been number one for decades now.

If you read a guidebook to dog breeds or look up their listing in a canine encyclopedia, you'll come across a succinct description of the Labrador retriever. It often reads something like this breed standard from the American Kennel Club:

> The Labrador Retriever is a strongly built, medium-sized, short-coupled, dog possessing a sound, athletic, well-balanced conformation that enables it to function as a retrieving gun dog; the substance and soundness to hunt waterfowl or upland game for long hours under difficult conditions; the character and quality to win in the show ring; and the temperament to be a family companion. . . . The ideal disposition is one of a kindly, outgoing, tractable nature; eager to please and non-aggressive towards man or animal. The Labrador has much that appeals to people; his gentle ways, intelligence and adaptability make him an ideal dog.

Yet as correct and endearing as that description is, it's still far from the everyday truth of the matter. As any owner of a Lab will tell you, each and every dog is in fact unique, practically a breed unto themselves.

And that's the joy of Labs.

A Brief History
of the
Labrador Retriever

*I*n North America, the rise of the Labrador retriever to the throne as one of our favorite dogs has come at a quick pace. The Lab didn't arrive in serious numbers in the United States until the 1920s and 1930s, although the breed enjoyed great popularity in Great Britain beginning in the early nineteenth century.

The Labrador retriever took a circuitous route to North American shores. The breed's origins lie up the eastern coast on the Canadian island of Newfoundland. The Labrador retriever was known there in the early nineteenth century as the Lesser Newfoundland or St. John's Newfoundland, and was a smaller cousin of today's Newfoundland breed. The St. John's Newfoundland earned its keep carrying lines between fishing vessels and from boats to shore. The hearty dogs carried the lines in heavy, North Atlantic seas, eagerly leaping into icy waters that would give a mere human hypothermia. At other times, they aided fishermen, hauling nets into boats or onto shore. They worked for their masters, serving a vital role in a rugged, unforgiving environment.

At some time around 1820, the second Earl of Malmesbury, a noted British sportsman of his day, is believed to have purchased several of these St. John's Newfoundlands from Newfoundland fishing boats docked at Poole Harbour in Dorset, England. At the time, English hunters were retrieving game primarily with pointers, setters, and water spaniels. But the superior talent for waterfowling of this imported Newfoundland breed quickly became apparent, and the dog gained rapid favor among British hunters. Colonel Peter Hawker, another leading sportsman of the era, is credited as the first to refer to the dogs as "Labradors," and the name stuck—even though the dogs did not actually come from the region of Labrador, Newfoundland's neighbor to the north.

The third earl of Malmesbury, James Howard Harris, wrote about his dogs in 1887 in a letter to a fellow sportsman: "We always call mine Labrador dogs and I have kept the breed as pure as I could from the first I had from Poole . . . known by their having a close coat which turns the water off like oil and, above all, a tail like an otter."

Others believe the name derives from the Spanish or Portuguese word for farm workers, "lavradores" or "labradores," respectively, where a breed of herding and guard dogs in the Portuguese village of Castro Laboreiro bear a resemblance to modern-day Labs and may have traveled a circuitous route to Canada with the famed Portuguese explorers.

The first yellow Lab on record was born in 1899, and named Ben of Hyde.

Around the turn of the century, Labs were brought back to North America, at first in small numbers. By 1930, the breed was winning many admirers in the United States, and a steady stream of dogs flowed into the country from Great Britain. The endearing qualities of this efficient working dog helped boost its popularity. In 1942, William F. Brown, editor of *The American Field*, wrote: "There is an external calmness about the dog that radiates confidence in his ability to do what is desired of him. A serenity of disposition that makes the Labrador an excellent companion. . . . Even those [Labs] which exude great keenness and fire, outwardly are imperturbable and seemingly seek to learn only what the master requires, then endeavor to do the job thoroughly, expeditiously."

The Lab is one of the oldest recognized breeds. The English Kennel Club first recognized the Labrador retriever as a distinct breed in 1903, and the American Kennel Club followed in 1917. Still, accurate pedigree papers for some of today's Labs can be traced as far back as 1878.

This first-class retriever with an unflappable, loyal personality quickly won the hearts of the Americans, just as it had of the British a century earlier and of the Newfoundland fishermen before that.

About
In Praise of Labs

We all have a favorite dog story. For some it's a childhood memory, a dog that grew up alongside us and was our best friend as we came of age. To others, it's the tale of a favorite dog's antics or their inherent intelligence—and sometimes, although not always, the two are combined. Then there are the stories of a dog that saved our life, an event that is quite common but by no means commonplace. And finally, there are the heartbreaking stories of a dog's passing, stories we tell over and over, not because they are favorites but simply as a way to soothe ourselves even now, years or decades or even a lifetime later.

In Praise of Labs collects together some favorite Lab stories. Here are tales by some of the world's greatest dog writers, such as Yorkshire veterinarian James Herriot and American dog lover, trainer, and writer Bill Tarrant. There's also an excerpt Gary Paulsen's reminiscence *My Life in Dog Years*, and humorist and folklorist Roger Welch's *A Life With Dogs*. And there's a bittersweet essay by "river rat" Kenny Salwey on the last days of one of his favorite dogs.

Combined together, these stories give praise where praise is due—to our Labrador retrievers.

Chapter 1

Of Dogs
and
Humans

"A Lab is a kind of perpetual five-year-old,
forever young, forever loving."
—James Michener

Dog and Man

The Story of a Great Friendship

by

Allyn Sloan and Arthur Farquhar

The history of treatises and poems chronicling our love for dogs

is a long one. Early sportsmen wrote about their favorite hunting

companions and great painters captured them in images.

In 1925, authors Allyn Sloan and Arthur Farquhar wrote

one of the most entertaining of all such treatises in their volume,

Dog and Man: The Story of a Great Friendship. Filled with

engravings of their favorite subject and published simultaneously

in London and New York, this was in truth a romantic tale.

This excerpt from the beginning of Sloan and Farquhar's

essay sets the stage for praising Labs—and indeed, all dogs.

This is the tale of a very great friendship which began many, many years ago, when Time was yet at its dawn. It is the tale of an enduring friendship which has braved the change of climates, time and customs, and is very much alive even to this day.

In this tale there are two central characters: first, Dog, because, according to tradition, he was created amongst the creatures early on the sixth day of God's creation; then, Man, for he was created, but later in that same day, to be a ruler over all the beasts of the earth.

Now, Dog is a word which comprises all varieties of the Dogkind, from those feathery-tailed, proud-spirited morsels of Chinese Royalty, the Pekingese, to the large, broad-headed, kindly-hearted St Bernard of the snowy heights of Helvetia.

Man is a term no less broad, for it includes the black and brown and yellow men of the East, and the white and red men of the West; and even as there are bad men and good men, kind and friendly men, as well as others cold and evil-hearted, so, besides our many loving and faithful friends, there are Dogs that delight to "bark and bite." But when you consider the example that some of us set them, can you blame them?

It is difficult to say exactly when Man and Dog became partners in the game of life—as difficult as it is to trace any great friendship to its root. Can you say when first you ceased to eye your friend with the cold, critical stare of acquaintance, and do you remember when first you saw him through the warm, kind eye of the heart? Probably on the day the seeds of love were planted, and since then the warmth of the sun of friendship has ripened that seed to maturity.

And so it came about between Man and Dog. But please do not forget that this all happened some little while ago—say 10,000 years or so—when Man was in the Neolithic stage of development, and not the stiff-shirted, top-hatted creature he is to-day. He and Dog met on a far more level footing, and, liking each other, struck a bargain and formed a very limited company of two. It probably happened somewhat after this fashion.

Man, having laboriously caught his food by digging a deep hole and covering it over with branches or brush and then waiting hungrily till some unwary beast fell into his trap, would eat it raw, pulling bone from bone, and would suck and pick, smacking his lips, happily unconscious of bad manners or present-day restrictions and conventions. Then, as each bone was picked clean, Man threw it out of his cave on to his midden or rubbish-heap, and, feeling brutishly happy, he would curl up with a grunt and go to sleep.

Outside in the dense darkness a pair of glowing yellow eyes had watched Man's doings, and those eyes had flashed a brighter gold when he saw those delicious bones thrown out on to the heap.

Seeing and hearing that Man slept, Dog (for it was none other than he) crept out of the undergrowth to negotiate the bone-pile, where he saw a meal worthy (to him) of the Ritz Restaurant. Of course, the bones had been pretty well picked by Man; still, they looked delicious; and so Dog gathered together his courage, which at first had oozed out of the very ends of his bristling coat, and stealthily advanced to the bone-heap. Nearer and nearer he crept; and then, with one sudden movement, he seized a nice, medium-sized bone and carried it back to his hiding-place beneath the forest trees.

Finding that Man slept on, Dog became more and more bold; and, as time went on, increasingly less cautious. At last he did not wait for the snoring evidence of Man's slumber, but prowled round the bone-heap all the time. It was probably in this way that Dog came into the habitation of Man. Gradually their bowing acquaintance ripened into something better, something close, for the seed of friendship and love to be sown.

So began the great partnership in the business of life, Dog brought to Man's use his scent, teeth, and so helped him to stalk, catch and kill his food. Man shared the food thus caught with his new friend, and invited him to sit beside him within the narrow circle of firelight, to give a feeling of companionship in that great unbroken silence of the early world. This feeling of warmth and friendliness towards Dog in Man was perhaps the first stirring of human kindness, friendship, and love in his wild, brutish heart; and it was surely then that the appealing, longing look first crept into Dog's hunted, wild gaze.

So they would sit, darkly silhouetted against the firelight, whilst all around them and over the sleeping world was purple night; and the only moving things that were seen were the shining stars which leapt and twinkled to the tune played by the dancing flames of Man's fire.

It's a Dog's Life

by

Gene Hill

Gene Hill is a long-time contributing editor to *Field & Stream*, and over the years, his writings have become as comfortable as old hunting boots. He's a relaxing storyteller, fitting for a cold winter night spent deep in a favorite chair near the hearth with your Lab asleep at your feet. He is a most human hunter and writes with humility of his often less-than-successful trips afield. Through his struggles, his readers can see themselves.

Gene's monthly *Field & Stream* "Hill Country" column reaches a wide audience. He is the author of many books, including *A Hunter's Fireside Book, Mostly Tailfeathers, A Listening Walk . . . and Other Stories,* and *Tears and Laughter: A Couple of Dozen Dog Stories.*

Gene is also a Labrador owner, and stories about the breed appear frequently in his writing. Whether it is puppies chewing up his favorite shoes, a field-trial champion pursuing a double retrieve, or an old-timer Lab sleeping on the rug, there always seems to be a Lab underfoot. This story is a word of warning—that many of us will blissfully overlook in favor of our Labs.

*N*o matter how much you paid for that doggie in the window, it's nothing compared to the cost of keeping him.

I recently found a newspaper clipping that claimed to estimate what it costs to own a dog. Based on a life expectancy of eleven years, the total came to about $13,000—not counting the cost of the dog. The expenses broke down as follows: food, $4,500; vet bills, $3,300; training, $2,000; grooming supplies, $1,200; collars, toys, and leashes, another $1,200; and flea and bug stuff $900.

I suppose that's accurate for an average non-sporting dog. But as the owner of various hunting dogs, I'd like to offer an additional list of items you could call "miscellaneous." If you're a gun dog owner, your list might deviate somewhat, but probably not by much. I'll leave it to you to fill in the costs.

Lab puppy: free, given to me by a friend who bought it at a DU dinner and, on sober reflection, decided against adding it to his household. New station wagon to transport dog, and kennel for same. House kennel (still unused), dog dish, dog bed. Training dummies, whistles, dummy launcher, blank cartridge pistol with holster. Hip boots, waders. New farm complete with pond. Boat for pond. Books on Lab training. Books telling what wonderful dogs Labs are. Lab prints, glasses with Labs on them. Lab doormat in case strangers didn't hear the racket that ensued at the ring of the doorbell. Field trial clubs with accompanying dues. New 12-gauge to serve as trial gun. New 12-gauge for duck shooting. New wardrobe for field trials and duck hunts.

After the dog is six months old, growth requires these items: new leashes, collars, and dummies. Sessions with professional trainer; travel to other trial grounds for participation and observation. Neckties with Labs on them. Upholstery repair for station wagon. Dog bed for wagon. New 20-gauge for upland gunning with Lab; new wardrobe for same.

At a year or year and a half, the expenses seem to level off. Normal wear and tear necessitates replacing some items, but these expenses are nothing you can't handle by making such simple sacrifices as cutting out restaurants, forgoing name-brand beverages at home, and discovering tasty tuna helpers and meat substitutes.

At this point many Lab owners, myself included, suffer a form of amnesia or mental derangement known medically as *multi-canis,* the seriousness of which varies. The addition of one Lab is the most common result, but acquisitions of two or three are commonly observed. Curiously, the victim

seems content, and may appear normal to all but the immediate family. Second mortgages are not uncommon at this stage.

Perversely, the worst thing that can happen to a Lab owner is that one or more of the dogs shows field trial promise. If this happens, large four-wheel-drive vehicles and dog trailers are thrown into the balance. Phone bills for calls to famous trainers resemble the annual budget of the welfare program the afflicted dog owner seems destined for. Maps with directions to remote and desolate swamps decorate the kitchen table where nourishing food was once served. Birthday and anniversary dates are replaced in the memory by pedigrees and blood-line characteristics; the vet doubles as the family doctor.

Then you must consider the following: upholstered chairs gutted because of curiosity or dissatisfaction; expensive shrubs and flowers excavated for the same reason. Rugs, blankets, pillows, chairs, boots, shoes, decoys, lamp cords, gloves, and books used for teething. Gifts to frightened delivery persons. New door screening and paint. Replacing wallpaper soaked by flying spray from wet coats. Glassware and china swept off tables by wagging tails. Removal of dog hair from moving parts of washer, drier, and refrigerator. Gifts to cat-owning neighbor.

To be honest, I'd guess that my Labs cost almost as much per year to raise and keep as a child, but this is hard to quantify. Both exhibit roughly the same table manners, but one marks doubles better than the other. Labs are easier to housebreak, but children can learn to do helpful chores. Generally, it's a wash.

I'm not going to discuss pointing dogs, since my experience with them is limited, but it would be foolish to think that, as with the Labs, anything less than a third of your annual income (net) could suffice. If you think I jest, remember that a lot of pointing dog country is in the South, where it's practically law that if you have a couple of high- stepping pointers, you need a high-stepping horse to complete the picture—or at least a high-stepping four-wheel-drive.

Finally, I'm sure you have often heard the old expression "going to the dogs." Remember the picture it conjures? Some poor soul in tatters and bent by care . . . not an inaccurate portrait of myself your faithful scrivener, toiling by guttering candlelight for the means to purchase a few bones, and hoping that when the dogs are through, there'll be something left for my soup.

"I no longer train my dogs. I imprint with them and they train themselves. You do the same and yours will too.
—Bill Tarrant, *Retriever Pups*

The Bonded, or Imprinted, Dog

by

Bill Tarrant

For more than a quarter century, Bill Tarrant was the Gun Dog Editor for *Field & Stream*, and his writings on Labrador retrievers and other hunting dogs have become beloved among dog fans.

Above all, Bill was perhaps the strongest voice anywhere for the humane treatment of dogs in training. An outspoken critic of training with intimidation, Bill based his beliefs not only on morality but also on results. He unequivocally declared that "domination in gun dog training is dead" and added that if a trainer bonds with his dog, "a look of disappointment on the trainer's face hurts an errant dog more than if he had been beat down with a 2 x 4."

In addition to hundreds of columns for the magazine, Bill was the author of eleven books, including *Bill Tarrant's Gun Dog Book: A Treasury of Happy Tails* and *Gun Dog Training: New Strategies from Today's Top Trainers*.

This excerpt from his last book, *Retriever Pups: The Formative First Year* (1999), serves as an ideal introduction Bill's philosophy—and as a mantra for all Lab owners.

Webster's new World Dictionary:

BOND: A binding or uniting force; tie; link. Anything that binds, fastens, or restrains.

IMPRINTING: A learning mechanism operating very early in the life of an animal, in which a particular stimulus immediately establishes an irreversible behavior pattern with reference to the same stimulus in the future.

And that stimulus is you.

*a*bsolute Warning: If you can't give thirty days to the infant pup—four to five weeks old at adoption—then there's no way you can imprint. You may bond but not imprint. Also there is this: To every rule there is the exception. Jim Culbertson's little black bitch, Keg of Black Powder, was the greatest Labrador retriever I ever saw or ever will see.

Yet, she was rejected as a pup; lived nine months without stimulus in her home kennel; was then adopted by Jim, who had never trained a Lab in his life; and she became the greatest hunter I ever popped a cap over and won both her open and amateur field trial championships.

So go with what I say but know that there's nothing ironclad under the sun.

The pup that imprints has got to be in a kennel crate at eye level when you're sleeping in bed. It is you who must awaken, however, as many times a night that is required to take him or her outdoors to tinkle. The pup has to be at your feet when you eat, at your side when reading the newspaper or watching TV, beside you in your vehicle when you run an errand.

He must be taken to field where he can run and snoop, you must maintain a supply of various game birds at all time. The pup must have complete access to your house and home; he must be able to look up or sniff around and find you at all times.

He must have unlimited play time with you—in the play is his future work.

Then and only then will you imprint.

Therefore, you cannot attempt to approach this halfway or part-time and accomplish a gun dog that is your duplicate in psyche, mind, body, and soul. When you walk, the pup walks. When you sigh, the pup sighs. He is you. Your clone. Your Siamese twin.

This is the dog that when you decide the birds are in the hedge row

to the left—he will cast left.

When you think there's ducks on the pond and drop to your knees, sneaking forward—he will sneak forward, too.

With no discussion, no prompting.

For he is you. One heart, one mind, one purpose.

And he reads your mind, near or afar. He knows what you're thinking sometimes before you do. He becomes mystical and beyond comprehension.

Like Jim Pettijohn's Labrador Booze. Jim was a pilot for TWA. In the beginning of his career he bid for flights and got the leavings, so his wife, Gloria, never knew where Jim had flown or when he was coming home. But up to two days before even Jim knew his schedule, Booze would take his place at the door of their home. Booze knew.

That's the gun dog I want for you.

I have been blessed with imprinted dogs the past twenty years. They are a humbling experience and they are a great obligation, for they have given their life to you, and you must care for that life and respect that life.

They cannot think any other way than you do, so you think only in ways to please them, to help them, to cherish them.

No way could you shock, shoot, kick, strike, or in any way punish this dog. He is helpless, for everything he is has been handed over to you. He is defenseless.

But then it would never come to pass you'd have to correct this dog, for he is so interpretive of your mind, he can only do what you're thinking.

Therefore this is the new age of gun dog training, the ultimate result. Those who still resort to dominance, pain, and exasperation are to be pitied, but not so much as their dogs, for their dogs are the helpless victims.

*N*ow you can bond, and that's great, too. Not as ironclad as imprinting, but still better than just training a dog the old-fashioned way and then taking him hunting.

You can bond with a dog adopted at seven weeks. You can bond with a dog with only part of your time spent in imprinting.

And this is probably the reality for you.

For you do not work at home, so you don't have all this time to "be" with Pup. And you're not there for all the little special things, like eating lunch, then telling Pup to jump in the truck and driving him around the block.

Or stopping at the Dairy Queen and buying him an ice cream cone. You'll be amazed at what a little act of kindness will accomplish.

I remember fifteen years ago when Terry Smith of Decaturville, Tennessee, and I were going duck hunting and we stopped at a McDonald's and bought each dog a Big Mac. It was only one bite apiece, but you from should have seen the joy in their eyes. And it's always a joy that's paid back. Those Labs did glomp the mud on that hunt.

Except for your spouse, that dog is the best friend you've got. Don't let him down. Always think of a kindness to give him. For that's exactly the way he thinks regarding you.

And remember: with any dog the miracle of an imprinted pup nears the realm of magic. The wand we use to touch the star and make it dazzle is YOU.

From
An History of the Earth and Animated Nature

by

Oliver Goldsmith

Irish naturalist, physician, and author Oliver Goldsmith is best known for his 1766 novel *The Vicar of Wakefield* and his 1771 play *She Stoops to Conquer*, standards of most university classes on English literature. Yet he was also a keen naturalist who sought to draw together all contemporary knowledge about the planet earth and its natural history, from the smallest plants to the largest animals. He published his research in the massive eight-volume encyclopedia *An History of the Earth and Animated Nature*, which first appeared in London in 1774. Among the entries, naturally, was a short treatise on the canine kind.

Reading Goldsmith's section on dogs, it's obvious that he was a great fan, and he often let his emotions get away from him. This shows up in his flowery writing style, waxing poetic on dogs and their behavior in a book that is supposedly pure science.

No matter. Goldsmith's treatise on dogs is just as true as if it were written yesterday.

Of all this tribe, the preferences being the most intelligent of all known quadrupeds and the acknowledged friend of mankind. The dog, independent of the beauty of his form, his vivacity, force and swiftness, is possessed of all those internal qualifications that can conciliate the affections of man, and make the tyrant a protector. A natural share of courage, and angry and ferocious disposition renders the dog, in its savage state, a formidable enemy to all other animals: but these readily give way to very different qualities in the domestic dog, whose only ambition seems the desire to please; he is seen to come crouching along, to lay his force, his courage, and all his useful talents, at the feet of his master; he waits his orders, to which he pays implicit obedience; he consults his looks, and a single glance is sufficient to put him in motion; he is more faithful even than the most boasted among men; he is constant in his affection, friendly without interest, and grateful for the slightest favours; much more mindful of benefits received, than injuries offered; he is not driven off by unkindness; he still continues humble, submissive, and imploring; his only hope to be serviceable; his only tenor to displease; he licks the hand that has just lifted to strike him, and at last disarms resentment, by submissive perseverance.

More docile than man, more obedient than any other animal, he is not only instructed in a short time, but he also conforms to the dispositions and the manners of those who command him. He takes his tone from the house he inhabits. When at night the guard of the house is committed to his care, he seems proud of the charge, he continues a watchful sentinel, he goes his rounds, scents strangers at a distance, and gives warning of his being upon duty. If they attempt to break in upon his territories, he becomes more fierce, flies at them, threatens, fights, and either conquers alone, or alarms those who have most interest in coming to his assistance; however, when he

has conquered, he quietly reposes upon his spoils, and abstains from what he has deterred others from abusing; giving thus at once a lesson of courage, temperance, and fidelity.

The dog, thus trusted, exerts a degree of superiority over all animals that require human protection. The flock and the herd obey his voice more readily even than that of the shepherd or the herdsman; he conducts them, guards them, keeps them from capriciously seeking danger, and their enemies he considers his own. Nor is he less useful in the pursuits; when the sound of the horn, or the voice of the huntsman calls him to the field, he testifies his pleasure by every little art, and pursues with perseverance, those animals, which, when taken, he must not expect to divide.

Few quadrupeds are less delicate in their food; and yet there are many kinds of birds which the dog will not venture to touch. It should seem that water is more necessary to the dog than food; he drinks often, though not abundantly; and it is commonly believed, that when abridged in water, he runs mad. This dreadful malady, the consequences of which are so well known, is the greatest inconvenience that results from the keeping this faithful domestic.

The Dustbin Dog

by

James Herriot

James Herriot was well into his fifties when he wrote his first memoir of his Yorkshire veterinarian practice. Since the publication of *All Creatures Great and Small* in the 1970s, his wonderful essays and his stories for children have made him one of the most cherished writers of the twentieth century.

Scottish by birth, Herriot practiced veterinary medicine in Yorkshire, where he also wrote most of his books, including *All Things Bright and Beautiful*, *All Things Wise and Wonderful*, *The Lord God Made Them All*, *Every Living Thing*, and *James Herriot's Yorkshire*. His children's books include *Moses the Kitten*, *Only One Woof*, and *The Market Square Dog*. Herriot always portrayed the animals he wrote about in a humane and loving voice.

This selection originally appeared in *The Lord God Made Them All* and was later published in *James Herriot's Dog Stories*. The tale features the awkward and goofy yellow Lab Brandy, who was replete with classic Labrador antics.

*I*n the semidarkness of the surgery passage I thought it was a hideous growth dangling from the side of the dog's face, but as he came closer, I saw that it was only a condensed milk can. Not that condensed milk cans are commonly found sprouting from dogs' cheeks, but I was relieved because I knew I was dealing with Brandy again. I hoisted him onto the table. "Brandy, you've been at the dustbin again."

The big golden Labrador gave me an apologetic grin and did his best to lick my face. He couldn't manage it since his tongue was jammed inside the can, but he made up for it by a furious wagging of tail and rear end.

"Oh, Mr. Herriot, I am sorry to trouble you again." Mrs. Westby, his attractive young mistress, smiled ruefully. "He just won't keep out of that dustbin. Sometimes the children and I can get the cans off ourselves, but this one is stuck fast. His tongue is trapped under the lid."

"Yes . . . yes . . ." I eased my finger along the jagged edge of the metal. "It's a bit tricky, isn't it? We don't want to cut his mouth."

As I reached for a pair of forceps, I thought of the many other occasions when I had done something like this for Brandy. He was one of my patients, a huge, lolloping, slightly goofy animal, but this dustbin raiding was becoming an obsession.

He liked to fish out a can and lick out the tasty remnants, but his licking was carried out with such dedication that he burrowed deeper and deeper until he got stuck. Again and again he had been freed by his family or myself from fruit salad cans, corned beef cans, baked bean cans, soup cans. There didn't seem to be any kind of can he didn't like.

I gripped the edge of the lid with my forceps and gently bent it back along its length till I was able to lift it away from the tongue. An instant later, that tongue was slobbering all over my cheek as Brandy expressed his delight and thanks.

"Get back, you daft dog!" I said, laughing, as I held the panting face away from me.

"Yes, come down, Brandy." Mrs. Westby hauled him from the table and spoke sharply. "It's all very fine, making a fuss now, but you're becoming a nuisance with this business. It will have to stop."

The scolding had no effect on the lashing tail, and I saw that his mistress was smiling. You just couldn't help liking Brandy because he was a great ball of affection and tolerance, without an ounce of malice in him.

I had seen the Westby children—there were three girls and a boy—

carrying him around by the legs, upside down, or pushing him in a pram, sometimes dressed in baby clothes. Those youngsters played all sorts of games with him, but he suffered them all with good humour. In fact, I am sure he enjoyed them.

Brandy had other idiosyncracies, apart from his fondness for dustbins.

I was attending the Westby cat at their home one afternoon when I noticed the dog acting strangely. Mrs. Westby was sitting, knitting in an armchair, while the oldest girl squatted on the hearth rug with me and held the cat's head.

It was when I was searching my pockets for my thermometer that I noticed Brandy slinking into the room. He wore a furtive air as he moved across the carpet and sat down with studied carelessness in front of his

mistress. After a few moments he began to work his rear end gradually up the front of the chair towards her knees. Absently, she took a hand away from her knitting and pushed him down, but he immediately restarted his backward ascent. It was an extraordinary mode of progression, his hips moving in a very slow rumba rhythm as he elevated them inch by inch, and all the time the golden face was blank and innocent, as though nothing at all were happening.

Fascinated, I stopped hunting for my thermometer and watched. Mrs. Westby was absorbed in an intricate part of her knitting and didn't seem to notice that Brandy's bottom was now firmly parked on her shapely knees which were clad in blue jeans. The dog paused, as though acknowledging that phase one had been successfully completed, then ever so gently he began to consolidate his position, pushing his way up the front of the chair with his fore limbs, till at one time he was almost standing on his head.

It was at that moment, just when one final backward heave would have seen the great dog ensconced on her lap, that Mrs. Westby finished the tricky bit of knitting and looked up.

"Oh, really, Brandy, you are silly!" She put a hand on his rump and sent him slithering disconsolately to the carpet, where he lay and looked at her with liquid eyes.

"What was all that about?" I asked.

Mrs. Westby laughed. "Oh, it's these old blue jeans. When Brandy first came here as a tiny puppy, I spent hours nursing him on my knee, and I used to wear the jeans a lot then. Ever since, even though he's a grown dog, the very sight of the things makes him try to get on my knee."

"But he doesn't just jump up?"

"Oh, no," she said. "He's tried it and got ticked off. He knows perfectly well I can't have a huge Labrador in my lap."

"So now it's the stealthy approach, eh?"

She giggled. "That's right. When I'm preoccupied—knitting or reading—sometimes he manages to get nearly all the way up, and if he's been playing in the mud he makes an awful mess, and I have to go and change. That's when he really does receive a scolding."

A patient like Brandy added colour to my daily round. When I was walking my own dog, I often saw him playing in the fields by the river. One particularly hot day many of the dogs were taking to the water, either to chase sticks or just to cool off, but whereas they glided in and swam off sedately, Brandy's approach was quite unique.

I watched as he ran up to the river bank, expecting him to pause before entering. But, instead, he launched himself outwards, legs splayed in a sort of swallow dive, and hung for a moment in the air rather like a flying fox before splashing thunderously into the depths. To me it was the action of a completely happy extrovert.

On the following day in those same fields I witnessed something even more extraordinary. There is a little children's playground in one corner—a few swings, a roundabout and a slide. Brandy was disporting himself on the slide.

For this activity he had assumed an uncharacteristic gravity of expression and stood calmly in the queue of children. When his turn came he mounted the steps, slid down the metal slope, all dignity and importance, then took a staid walk round to rejoin the queue.

The little boys and girls who were his companions seemed to take him for granted, but I found it difficult to tear myself away. I could have watched him all day.

I often smiled to myself when I thought of Brandy's antics, but I didn't smile when Mrs. Westby brought him into the surgery a few months later. His bounding ebullience had disappeared, and he dragged himself along the passage to the consulting room.

As I lifted him onto the table, I noticed that he had lost a lot of weight.

"Now, what is the trouble, Mrs. Westby?" I asked.

She looked at me worriedly. "He's been offcolour for a few days now, listless and coughing and not eating very well, but this morning he seems quite ill, and you can see he's starting to pant."

"Yes . . . yes . . . " As I inserted the thermometer I watched the rapid rise and fall of the rib cage and noted the gaping mouth and anxious eyes. "He does look very sorry for himself."

Temperature was 104. I took out my stethoscope and ausculated his lungs. I have heard of an old Scottish doctor describing a seriously ill patient's chest as sounding like a "kist o' whustles" and that just about described Brandy's. Râles, wheezes, squeaks and bubblings—they were all there against a background of laboured respiration.

I put the stethoscope back in my pocket. "He's got pneumonia."

"Oh, dear." Mrs. Westby reached out and touched the heaving chest. "That's bad, isn't it?"

"Yes, I'm afraid so."

"But . . . " She gave me an appealing glance. "I understand it isn't so fatal since the new drugs came out."

I hesitated. "Yes, that's quite right. In humans and most animals the sulpha drugs, and now penicillin, have changed the picture completely, but dogs are still very difficult to cure."

Thirty years later it is still the same. Even with all the armoury of antibiotics that followed penicillin—streptomycin, the tetracyclines, the synthetics and the new nonantibiotic drugs and steroids—I still hate to see pneumonia in a dog.

"But you don't think it's hopeless?" Mrs. Westby asked.

"No, no, not at all. I'm just warning you that so many dogs don't respond to treatment when they should. But Brandy is young and strong. He must stand a fair chance. I wonder what started this off, anyway."

"Oh, I think I know, Mr. Herriot. He had a swim in the river about a week ago. I try to keep him out of the water in this cold weather, but if he sees a stick floating, he just takes a dive into the middle. You've seen him—it's one of the funny little things he does."

"Yes, I know. And was he shivery afterwards?"

"He was. I walked him straight home, but it was such a freezingcold day. I could feel him trembling as I dried him down."

I nodded. "That would be the cause, all right. Anyway, let's start his treatment. I'm going to give him this injection of penicillin, and I'll call at your house tomorrow to repeat it. He's not well enough to come to the surgery."

"Very well, Mr. Herriot. And is there anything else?"

"Yes, there is. I want you to make him what we call a pneumonia jacket. Cut two holes in an old blanket for his forelegs and stitch him into it along his back. You can use an old sweater if you like, but he must have his chest warmly covered. Only let him out in the garden for necessities."

I called and repeated the injection on the following day. There wasn't much change. I injected him for four more days, and the realisation came to me sadly that Brandy was like so many of the others—he wasn't responding. The temperature did drop a little, but he ate hardly anything and grew gradually thinner. I put him on sulphapyridine tablets, but they didn't seem to make any difference.

As the days passed and he continued to cough and pant and to sink deeper into a blankeyed lethargy, I was forced more and more to a conclusion which, a few weeks ago, would have seemed impossible—that this happy, bounding animal was going to die.

But Brandy didn't die. He survived. You couldn't put it any higher than that. His temperature came down and his appetite improved, and he climbed onto a plateau of twilight existence where he seemed content to stay.

"He isn't Brandy anymore," Mrs. Westby said one morning a few weeks later when I called in. Her eyes filled with tears as she spoke.

I shook my head. "No, I'm afraid he isn't. Are you giving him the halibut liver oil?"

"Yes, every day. But nothing seems to do him any good. Why is he like this, Mr. Herriot?"

"Well, he has recovered from a really virulent pneumonia, but it's left him with a chronic pleurisy, adhesions and probably other kinds of lung damage. It looks as though he's just stuck there."

She dabbed at her eyes. "It breaks my heart to see him like this. He's only five, but he's like an old, old dog. He was so full of life, too." She sniffed and blew her nose. "When I think of how I used to scold him for getting into the dustbins and muddying up my jeans. How I wish he would do some of his funny old tricks now."

I thrust my hands deep into my pockets. "Never does anything like that now, eh?"

"No, no, just hangs about the house. Doesn't even want to go for a walk."

As I watched, Brandy rose from his place in the corner and pottered slowly over to the fire. He stood there for a moment, gaunt and deadeyed, and he seemed to notice me for the first time because the end of his tail gave a brief twitch before he coughed, groaned and flopped down on the hearth rug.

Mrs. Westby was right. He was like a very old dog.

"Do you think he'll always be like this?" she asked.

I shrugged. "We can only hope."

But as I got into my car and drove away, I really didn't have much hope. I had seen calves with lung damage after bad pneumonias. They recovered but were called "bad doers" because they remained thin and listless for the rest of their lives. Doctors, too, had plenty of "chesty" people on their books; they were, more or less, in the same predicament.

Weeks and then months went by, and the only time I saw the Labrador was when Mrs. Westby was walking him on his lead. I always had the impression that he was reluctant to move, and his mistress had to stroll along very slowly so that he could keep up with her. The sight of him saddened me when I thought of the lolloping Brandy of old, but I told myself that at least I had saved his life. I could do no more for him now, and I made a determined effort to push him out of my mind.

In fact, I tried to forget Brandy and managed to do so fairly well until one afternoon in February. On the previous night I felt I had been through the fire. I had treated a colicky horse until 4 A.M. and was crawling into bed, comforted by the knowledge that the animal was settled down and free from pain, when I was called to a calving. I had managed to produce a large

Chapter 2

Family Friend

"No one can fully understand the meaning of love unless he's owned a dog. He can show you more honest affection with a flick of his tail than a man can gather through a lifetime of handshakes."
—Gene Hill, "The Dog Man" from *Tears & Laughter*, 1981

From the Wild

by

Ted Kerasote

Ted Kerasote's essays on nature, travel, and the environment have appeared in more than fifty periodicals, including *Audubon*, *Outside*, and *National Geographic Traveler*. He's the author of four books, including 2004's *Out There*, which was a winner of the National Outdoor Book Award for literature. His expeditions have taken him to the mountains and rivers of six continents.

This excerpt is from Kerasote's 2007 book *Merle's Door: Lessons from a Freethinking Dog*.

Kerasote found Merle, a Labrador retriever mix, while on a camping trip. Merle had been living in the wild, and after taking the dog home with him, Kerasote soon realized that Merle could not adjust to living exclusively in the human world. So, he put a door in his house to let Merle live both indoors and run free in the wild.

*H*e came out of the night, appearing suddenly in my headlights, a big, golden dog, panting, his front paws tapping the ground in an anxious little dance. Behind him, tall cottonwoods in their April bloom. Behind the grove, the San Juan River, moving quickly, dark and swollen with spring melt.

It was nearly midnight, and we were looking for a place to throw down our sleeping bags before starting our river trip in the morning. Next to me in the cab of the pickup sat Benj Sinclair, at his feet a midden of road-food wrappers smeared with the scent of corn dogs, onion rings, and burritos. Round-cheeked, Buddha-bellied, thirty-nine years old, Benj had spent his early years in the Peace Corps, in West Africa, and had developed a stomach that could digest anything. Behind him in the jump seat was Kim Reynolds, an Outward Bound instructor from Colorado known for her grace in a kayak and her long braid of brunette hair, which held the faint odor of a healthy, thirty-two-year-old woman who had sweated in the desert and hadn't used deodorant. Like Benj and me, she had eaten a dinner of pizza in Moab, Utah, a hundred miles up the road where we'd met her. Like us, she gave off the scents of garlic, onions, tomato sauce, basil, oregano, and anchovies.

In the car that pulled up next to us were Pam Weiss and Bennett Austin. They had driven from Jackson Hole, Wyoming, to Moab in their own car, helped us rig the raft and shop for supplies, joined us for pizza, and, like us, wore neither perfume nor cologne. Pam was thirty-six, an Olympic ski racer, and Bennett, twenty-five, was trying to keep up with her. They had recently fallen in love and exuded a mixture of endorphins and pheromones.

People almost never describe other people in these terms—noting first their smells—for we're primarily visual creatures and rely on our eyes for information. By contrast, the only really important sense-key for the big, golden dog, doing his little dance in the headlights, was our olfactory signatures, wafting to him as we opened the doors.

It was for this reason—smell—that I think he trotted directly to my door, leaned his head forward cautiously, and sniffed at my bare thigh. What mix of aromas went up his long snout at that very first moment of our meeting? What atavistic memories, what possibilities were triggered in his canine worldview as he untangled the mysteries of my sweat?

The big dog—now appearing reddish in the interior light of the truck and without a collar—took another reflective breath and studied me with excited consideration. Might it have been what I ate, and the subtle residue

it left in my pores, that made him so interested in me? It was the only thing I could see (note my human use of "see" even while describing an olfactory phenomenon) that differentiated me from my friends. Like them, I skied, biked, and climbed, and was single. I had just turned forty-one, a compact man with chestnut hair and bright brown eyes. But when I ate meat, it was that of wild animals, not domestic ones—mostly elk and antelope along with the occasional grouse, duck, goose, and trout mixed in.

Was it their metabolized essence that intrigued him—some whiff of what our Paleolithic ancestors had shared? Smell is our oldest sense. It was the olfactory tissue at the top of our primeval nerve cords that evolved into our cerebral hemispheres, where thought is lodged. Perhaps the dog—a being who lived by his nose—knew a lot more about our connection than I could possibly imagine.

His deep brown eyes looked at me with luminous appreciation and said, "You need a dog, and I'm it."

Unsettled by his uncanny read of me—I had been looking for a dog for over a year—I gave him a cordial pat and replied, "Good dog."

His tail beat steadily, and he didn't move, his eyes still saying, "You need a dog."

As we got out of the cars and began to unpack our gear, I lost track of him. There was his head, now a tail, there a rufous flank moving among bare legs and sandals.

I threw my pad and bag down on the sand under a cottonwood, slipped into its silky warmth, turned over, and found him digging a nest by my side. Industriously, he scooped out the sand with his front paws, casting it between his hind legs before turning, turning, turning, and settling to face me. In the starlight, I could see one brow go up, the other down.

Of course, "brows" isn't really the correct term, since dogs sweat only through their paws and have no need of brows to keep perspiration out of their eyes, as we do. Yet, certain breeds of dogs have darker hair over their eyes, what might be called "brow markings," and he had them.

The Hidatsa, a Native American tribe of the northern Great Plains, believe that these sorts of dogs, whom they call "Four-Eyes," are especially gentle and have magical powers. Stanley Coren, the astute canine psychologist from the University of British Columbia, has also noted that these "four-eyed" dogs obtained their reputation for psychic powers "because their expressions were easier to read than those of other dogs. The contrasting-colored spots make the movements of the muscles over the eye much more visible."

In the starlight, the dog lying next to me raised one brow while lowering the other, implying curiosity mixed with concern over whether I'd let him stay.

"Night," I said, giving him a pat. Then I closed my eyes.

W hen I opened them in the morning, he was still curled in his nest, looking directly at me.

"Hey," I said.

Up went one brow, down went the other.

"I am yours," his eyes said.

I let out a breath, unprepared for how his sweet, faintly hound-dog face—going from happiness to concern—left a cut under my heart. I had been looking at litters of Samoyeds, balls of white fur with bright black mischievous eyes. The perfect breed for a winter person like myself, I thought. But I couldn't quite make myself bring one home. I had also seriously considered Labrador Retrievers, taken by their exuberant personalities and knowing that such a robust, energetic dog could easily share my life in the outdoors as well as be the bird dog I believed I wanted. But no Lab pup had given me that undeniable heart tug that said, "We are a team."

The right brow of the dog lying by me went down as he held my eye. His left brow went up, implying, "You delayed with good reason."

"Maybe," I said, feeling my desire for a pedigree dog giving way. "Maybe," I said once more to the dog whose eyes coasted across mine, returned, and lingered. He did have the looks of a reddish yellow Lab, I thought, at least from certain angles.

At the sound of my voice, he levered his head under my arm and brought his nose close to mine. Surprisingly, he didn't try to lick me in that effusive gesture that many dogs use with someone they perceive as dominant to them, whether it be a person or another dog—a relic, some believe, of young wolves soliciting food from their parents and other adult wolves. The adults, not having hands to carry provisions, bring back meat in their stomachs. The pups lick their mouths, and the adults regurgitate the partly digested meat. Pups who eventually become alphas abandon subordinate licking. Lower-ranking wolves continue to display the behavior to higher-ranking wolves, as do a great many domestic dogs to people. This dog's self-possession gave me pause. Was he not licking me because he considered us peers? Or did my body language—both of us being at the same level—allow him to feel somewhat of an equal? He circumspectly smelled my breath, and I, in turn, smelled his. His smelled sweet.

Whatever he smelled on mine, he liked it. "I am yours," his eyes said again.

Disconcerted by his certainty about me, I got up and moved off. I didn't want to abandon my plans for finding a pup who was only six to eight weeks old and whom I could shape to my liking. The dog read my energy and didn't follow me. Instead, he went to the others, greeting them with a wagging tail and wide laughs of his toothy mouth. "Good morning, good morning, did you sleep well?" he seemed to be saying.

But as I organized my gear, I couldn't keep my eyes from him. Despite his ribs showing, he appeared fit and strong, and looked like he had been living outside for quite a while, his hair matted with sprigs of grass and twigs. He was maybe fifty-five pounds, not filled out yet, his fox-colored fur hanging in loose folds, waiting for the adult dog that would be. He had a ridge of darker fur along his spine, short golden plumes on the backs of his legs, and a tuxedo-like bib of raised fur on his chest—just an outline of it—scattered with white flecks. His ears were soft and flannel-like, and hung slightly below the point of his jaw. His nose was lustrous black, he had equally shiny lips, and his teeth gleamed. His tail was large and powerful.

Every time I looked at him, he seemed to manifest his four-eyed ancestry, shape-shifting before me: now the Lab I wanted; there a Rhodesian Ridgeback, glinting under some faraway Kalahari sun; an instant later he became a long-snouted coydog, born of the redrock desert and brought to life out of these canyons and cacti. When he looked directly at me—one brow up, the other down, his cheeks creased in concern—he certainly appeared to have some hound in him. Obviously, he had belonged to someone, for his testicles were gone and the scar of neutering had completely healed and the hair had grown back.

As I cooked breakfast at one of the picnic tables, he rejoined me, sitting patiently a few feet away while displaying the best of manners as he watched the elk sausage go from my hands to the frying pan. He gave not a single whine, though a tiny tremor went through his body.

When the slices were done, I said, "Would you like some?"

A shiver ran through him once again. His eyes shone; but he didn't move. I broke off a piece and offered it to him. His nose wriggled in delight; he took it delicately from my fingertips and swallowed. His tail broomed the sand, back and forth in appreciation.

"That dog," said the Bureau of Land Management ranger who had come up to us and was checking our river permit as we ate, "has been hanging around here for a couple of days. I think he's abandoned, which is strange because he's beautiful and really friendly."

We all agreed he was.

"Where did he come from?" I asked her.

"He just appeared," she replied.

The dog watched this conversation carefully, looking from the ranger's face to mine.

I picked up a stick, wanting to see how well he could retrieve. The instant I drew back my arm, he cringed pathetically, retreated a few paces, and eyed me warily.

"He can be skittish," the ranger said. "I think someone's beat him."

I flung the stick away from him, toward the moving river. He gave it a cool appraisal, then looked at me, just as cool. "I don't fetch," the look said. "That's for dogs."

"He doesn't fetch," the ranger said.

"So I notice."

She checked our fire pan and our portable toilet—both required by the BLM for boaters floating the San Juan River—while the dog hung around nearby, hopeful but trying to look unobtrusive.

"I'd take that dog if I could," the ranger said, noting my eyes lingering on him. "But we're not allowed to have dogs."

"Maybe we should take him down the river," I heard myself say.

"I would," she said.

When I discussed it with the others, they agreed that we could use a mascot, a river dog, for our trip. Taking a dog on a wilderness excursion is hardly a new idea. In fact, it's a North American tradition. Alexander Mackenzie had a pickup mutt who accompanied him on his landmark first journey across the continent to the Pacific in 1793, via southern Canada. The dog was unnamed in Mackenzie's diary but often mentioned for surviving swims in rapids and killing bison calves. Meriwether Lewis also had a dog on his and William Clark's journey up the Missouri and down the Columbia from 1803 to 1806. The acclaimed Newfoundland Seaman protected camp from grizzlies and caught countless squirrels for the pot, as well as pulling down deer, pronghorn antelope, and geese. Although the expedition ate dozens of other dogs when game became scarce (they were bought from Indians), there was never a question of grilling Seaman. An honored member of the expedition to the end, he may have kept the depression-prone Lewis sane on the arduous journey. Three years after returning to civilization, unable to reintegrate into society, and with no mention of what happened to his dog, Lewis committed suicide. John James Audubon had a Newfie as well, a tireless hiker named Plato, who accompanied him across the countryside and retrieved many of the birds the artist shot for his paintings. Audubon called him "a well-trained and most sagacious animal."

With such august precedents, it would have seemed a shame not to take this handsome, well-behaved dog with us. What harm could come of it? No one raised the issue of what we'd do with him when we pulled out at Clay Hills above Lake Powell in six days. We'd cross that bridge when we came to it. In the meantime, this wasn't the nineteenth century. There'd be no living off the land; we needed to get him some dog food. Benj and I drove into the nearby town of Bluff, Utah, returning with a bag of Purina Dog Chow and a box of Milk Bones.

The only one who wasn't aware that the dog was going with us was, of course, the dog himself. After loading the raft with dry bags and coolers of food, I patted the gunwale and said to him, "Jump in. You're a river dog now." I had been designated to row the raft for the first day while the others paddled kayaks.

Dubiously, he eyed the raft. "No way," his eyes said, "that looks dangerous."

I tried to pet him, but he danced away, making a "ha-ha-ha" noise, half playful, half scared, as he pumped his front paws up and down in that energetic little dance he'd done the previous night as he appeared in our headlights.

"You'll like it," I said. "Shady canyons, great campsites, petroglyphs, swimming every day, Milk Bones, Purina Dog Chow, and"—my voice cajoled—"elk sausage."

I opened my waterproof lunch stuff sack, cut off a piece of the elk summer sausage, and held it out to him. He came closer, leaned his head forward, and snatched it. "Come on, jump in."

He shivered, knowing full well he was being gulled, but letting me pet him nonetheless, torn between wanting to come and his fear of the raft. Carefully, I put my arms around him, under his chest, and lifted. Whining in protest, he struggled. I managed to deposit him in the raft as Benj tried to push us off.

The dog leapt out of the boat, but instead of fleeing danced up and down the shore, panting frantically, "Ha-ha-ha, ha-ha-ha," which I translated as "I really want to go, but I don't know where we're going, and I don't like the raft, and I'm scared."

I talked to him in a low, soothing tone and got him calmed down enough so I could pet him again. Resting his head on my knee, he gave a huge sigh, like someone who's emotionally wrung out. For a moment, I could sense his many dashed hopes and his fear of people and their gear— not an unreasonable one given how he had cowered when I raised the stick to play fetch.

The others were in their kayaks, ready to go. Carefully, I got my arms around him again, but when I lifted him he struggled mightily, calling out in desperate whining yelps. I put him in the boat, and Benj shoved us off as I held the dog until the current took us. Then I let go of him and started to row. We were only yards from shore. With a leap and a few strokes he could easily return to land. Stay or leave—the choice was his. The dog jumped to the raft's gunwale, put his paws on it, and stared upstream without showing any fear of the moving water. Rather, he watched the retreating shore as if watching his natal continent disappear below the horizon.

His ambivalence filled my mind with questions. Had he been abandoned, or gotten himself lost? In either case, was he waiting faithfully for his human to return? Was his friendliness toward me his way of asking for my help in finding that person? Had I misread his eyes, seeming to say, "You are the one I've been waiting for"? Was his longing gaze back to shore simply his attachment to a known place—a familiar landscape where he might have been mistreated but which was still home? How many abused souls—dogs and humans alike—have remained in an unloving place because staying was far less terrifying than leaving?

"Easy, easy," I murmured as he began to tremble.

I stroked his head and shoulders. Turning, he looked at me with an expression I shall never forget. It mingled loss, fear of the unknown, and hope.

Of course, some will say that I was being anthropomorphic. Others might point out that I was projecting. But what I was doing—reading his body language—is the stock-in-trade of psychologists as they study their clients. All of us use the same technique as we try to understand the feelings of those around us—friends, family members, and colleagues. There'd be no human intercourse, or it would be enormously impoverished, without our attempting to use our own emotions as templates—as starting points—to map the feelings of others.

But something else was going on between the dog and me. An increasing amount of research on a variety of species—parrots, chimpanzees, prairie dogs, dolphins, wolves, and domestic dogs themselves—has demonstrated that they have the physical and cognitive ability to transmit a rich array of information to others, both within and without their species, sometimes even using grammatical constructions similar to those employed in human languages. Individuals of some of these species can also identify themselves with vocal signatures—in human terms, a name.

These studies have corroborated what I've felt about dogs for a long time—that they're speakers of a foreign language and, if we pay attention to their vocalizations, ocular and facial expressions, and ever-changing postures, we can translate what they're saying. Sometimes we get the translation spot-on ("I'm hungry"), sometimes we make a reasonable guess ("I'm sad"), and occasionally we have to use a figure of speech to bridge the divide between their culture and our own ("I love you so much, my heart could burst").

Dog owners who hold "conversations" with their dogs will know exactly what I mean. Those who don't—as well as those who find the whole notion of conversing with a dog absurd—may want to consider that humans have shared a longer and more intimate partnership with dogs than with any other domestic animal, starting before civilization existed. In these early times—before speech and writing achieved the ascendancy they enjoy today—dogs had a greater opportunity to make themselves understood by humans who were still comfortable communicating outside the boundaries of the spoken and written word.

Charles Darwin, as keen an observer of domestic dogs as he was of Galápagos finches, commented on the relative equality that once existed between dogs and humans, and still exists, if you look for it: "[T]he difference in mind between man and the higher animals, great as it is, certainly is one of degree and not of kind." Darwin went so far as to say that "there is no fundamental difference between man and the higher mammals in their mental faculties," adding that nonhuman animals experience happiness, wonder, shame, pride, curiosity, jealousy, suspicion, gratitude, and magnanimity. "They practice deceit and are revengeful," he asserted, and have "moral qualities," the more important elements of which are "love and the distinct emotion of sympathy." These were breathtaking notions when he set them down in 1871 and remain eye-opening today, even to many who believe that animals can think.

The dog now took his eyes from mine, looked back to the shore, and let out a resigned sigh—I was to learn that he was a great sigher. Stepping down into the raft, he gave our gear a brief inspection and finally let his gaze settle upon the cooler sitting in the bow of the raft, surrounded by dry bags. Padding over to it, he jumped on it and lay down with his back to me. Another sigh escaped him. Within a few moments, however, I could see him watching the bluffs and groves of cottonwoods with growing interest, his head snapping this way and that as he noted the countryside moving while he apparently did not.

"Pretty cool, eh?"

He moved his ears backward, acknowledging my voice without turning his head.

As we entered the first canyon, and its walls blocked out the sky, he took a glance upstream and gave a start—the campground had disappeared. He jerked into a sitting position and stared around apprehensively. Without warning, he pointed his snout to the sky and let out a mournful howl, beginning in a bass register and climbing to a plaintive alto crescendo. From the canyon walls came back his echo: "Aaawooo, Aaawooo, Aaawooo."

Stunned, he cocked his head at the unseen dog who had answered him. Where was the dog hiding? He looked up and down the river and at the high shadowed cliffs. He seemed never to have heard an echo before. A moment later, he howled again, and again he was surprised to hear his voice rebounding from the cliffs. He looked around uneasily before giving another howl—this time as a test rather than to bemoan his situation. When the echo returned, a look of dawning realization crossed his face. It was remarkable to see the comprehension light his eyes. His lips turned up in a smile, and he howled again, long and drawn out, but without any sadness. Immediately, he cocked his head to listen to his echo. As the canyon walls sent back his voice, he began to lash his tail back and forth with great enthusiasm. He turned around and gave me a look of surprised delight—the very same expression people wear when they hear themselves for the first time.

I leaned forward and put a hand on his chest.

"You are quite the singer," I told him.

Throwing back his head, he laughed a toothy grin.

From that moment on, he never looked back. He sat on the cooler like a sphinx, his head turning to watch the cliffs and side canyons go by. He hiked up to several Anasazi cliff dwellings with us and stood attentively as we examined petroglyphs. On the way back to the river, he'd meander off, disappearing for long minutes, only to reappear as we approached the boats, dashing toward us through the cactus without a glance at the obstacle course he was threading. He seemed about as home in the desert as a dog could be.

At camp that evening, he supervised our shuttling the gear from raft to higher ground and watched as we began to unpack our dry bags. Then, satisfied we weren't going to leave, he vanished. I caught glimpses of him, exploring a large perimeter around our campsite, poking with his paw at some object of interest, sniffing at bushes, and raising his leg to mark them. When I began to pour his dinner into one of our cooking pots, he soon appeared, having heard the tinkle of kibble on steel. Inhaling his dinner in a few voracious gulps, he looked up at me and wagged his tail. Cocking his head, he raised an eyebrow and clearly added, "Nice appetizer. Now where's the meal?"

I poured him some more, and after he gobbled it he gave me the same look: "Is that all?" Likewise after the next bowl.

"Enough," I told him, crossing my hands and moving them apart the way an umpire makes the signal for "Safe."

His face fell.

"We've got five more days," I explained. "You can't have it all tonight." Stowing his food, I said, "Come on, help me with the latrine."

He followed as I took the large ammo box inland and placed it on a rock bench with a scenic overlook of the river. After lining it with a stout plastic bag, I gave it its inaugural use as the dog sat a half dozen feet off, wagging his tail in appreciation as the aromas wafted toward him. Each day's bag had to be sealed and carried downriver to be disposed of properly at the end of the trip, and we had brought along a can of Comet to sprinkle on the contents so as to reduce the production of odors and methane. This I now did, leaving the can of Comet and the roll of toilet paper by the side of the ammo box. As I walked back to camp, the big golden dog followed me, his nose aloft, his nostrils dilating.

At dinnertime we sat in a circle around the stoves and pots, and the dog lay on his belly between Benj and me, looking alertly at each of us when we spoke. We were discussing what to call him besides "hey you."

Bennett proposed "Merlin," since the dog seemed to have some magic about him. Benj, who was opening a bottle of wine, wanted something connected to our trip, like, for instance, "Merlot." He poured us each a cup and offered some to the dog for a sniff. The dog pulled back his head in alarm and looked at the cup with disdain.

"Not a drinker," Benj commented.

"What about 'Hintza'?" I suggested. "He was the Rhodesian
Ridgeback in Laurens van der Post's novel *A Story Like the Wind*. He looks
like Hintza."

There were several attempts to call the dog Hintza, all of which
elicited a pained expression on his face, as if the vibratory second syllable,
"tza," might be causing him auditory distress. "So much for literary heroes,"
I said.

Someone threw out the name of the river, "San Juan." This brought
about universal nays.

The sky turned dusky, the stars came out, the river made its soothing
whoosh along the bank below us. We got into our sleeping bags. I watched
the still nameless dog pad down to the river, take a drink, then disappear. I
don't know how much later it was that I felt his back settle against mine.
He was warm and solid, and he gave a great, contented sigh.

He wasn't there in the morning, but appeared shortly after I woke.

Bounding toward me, he twirled around in excitement, pumping his front paws up and down and panting happily.

I roughed up his neck fur, and he closed his eyes in pleasure, going relaxed and easy under my hands.

We had breakfast and broke camp. Benj, who had been the last to use the latrine, carried it down to the beach. The dog was at his heels.

"I know what we can name him," Benj called out, twisting his face into an expression of disgust, "'Monsieur le Merde.' He ate the shit out of the ammo box."

"Ick," said Kim.

"No," I exclaimed in disbelief, watching the dog to see if he was foaming at the mouth or displaying some other sign of having been poisoned by the Comet. He looked absolutely tip-top, wagging his tail cheerfully.

"Are you sure, Benj?" I asked. "Did you actually see him eat it?"

"No, but it's empty, and who else would have done it? I saw him coming back from the latrine when I walked to it."

"He could have been someplace else." I knelt in the sand and said "come here" to the dog.

He came right up to me, and I leaned close and smelled his mouth. "Yuck!" I exploded, falling backward, as the stench overwhelmed me. "You are a vile dog."

He wagged his tail happily.

"You must be really hungry," I added.

"The question," said Pam, "is who's gonna row with him?"

We decided to draw straws, and Benj lost. "At least," he said, staring at the short straw, "someone on this trip has worse eating habits than me."

We headed downriver, the morning breeze cool, the sun sprinkling the wavelets with glister. As the canyon widened, opening upon a grassy shoreline, the dog sat up smartly on the cooler. A dozen or so head of cattle grazed along the left bank, raising their heads to watch us pass. They were Navajo cattle, the entire left bank of the San Juan River being the northern boundary of the Navajo Nation, which covers a sizeable portion of Utah, Arizona, and New Mexico.

The dog gave them a sharp, excited look, and leapt off the cooler. Flying through the air with his front and back legs extended, he hit the water in a mushroom of spray. His head surfaced and he began to paddle rapidly to the shore. Scrambling up the rocky bank, he shook himself once, and, as the cows watched in disbelief, he sprinted directly at them. They wheeled and galloped downriver.

Nose and tail extended, he chased after them, his wet coat flashing reddish-gold in the sunlight. Through willow and cactus he sprinted, closing the distance with remarkable speed and cutting out the smallest calf with an expert flanking movement. Coming abreast of the calf's hindquarter, he forced it away from the herd and toward the cliffs. It was clear he intended to corner it against the rocks and kill it.

Stunned, we watched in silence. Besides, what could we do? Yell, "Hey, dog, stop!"?

Yet something about his behavior told me that he hadn't totally lost himself to that hardwired state into which dogs disappear when they lock onto fleeing prey. Focused solely on the animal fleeing before them, they can run for miles, losing track of where they or their humans might be.

This dog wasn't doing that. As he coursed alongside the terrified calf, he kept glancing toward the raft and the kayaks, heading downriver to a bend that would take us out of sight. And I could see that he was calculating two mutually exclusive outcomes: the juicy calf and the approaching cliffs where he'd corner it, or the fast-retreating boats and the family he had found.

I saw him glance again at the bend of the river where we'd vanish—and right there I realized that dogs could think abstractly. The calf was as real as real could be, a potential meal right now.
The boat people, their Purina Dog Chow, and the affection they shared with him were no more than memories of the past and ideas about the future, or however these English words translate in the mind of a dog.

Instant gratification . . . future benefits. The choices seemed clear. And mind you, we weren't calling or waving to him. Without a word, we floated silently down the river.

He chose the future. He broke off his chase in midstride, cut right, streaking past the group of startled cows who had gathered in a protective huddle. Reaching the bank, he raced along its rocky apron, trying to gain as much ground on us as he could before having to swim. Faced by willow, he leapt—again legs stretched fore and aft, ears flapping like wings—before belly crashing into the water. Paddling with determination, he set a course downriver that would intercept our float.

After a long haul—mouth open, breathing hard, eyes riveted upon us—he reached Kim's boat, swam up to her gunwale, and tried to claw his way aboard. She grabbed the loose fur on his back and hauled him onto her spray skirt. He looked suddenly very thin and bedraggled, especially when he turned to gaze wistfully after the cows. He heaved a great sigh of disappointment when the cliffs cut them off from view, then turned to me, floating fifty feet off. Springing from Kim's boat, he swam to mine. I helped him aboard, and he stared into my face with what appeared to be distress.

"You look like you've done that before," I said.

His eyes coasted away from mine.

Sensing his guilt, I tried to praise him. "You're quite the swimmer."

For the first time, he leaned forward and licked my mouth—just once before jumping out of my arms and into the water.

The dunking had at least cleared his breath. He swam to the raft, allowing Benj to haul him in. Standing on the cooler, he shook himself vigorously, then reclined in his sphinx position to let the sun dry his fur.

Paddling up to the raft, I heard Benj talking to the dog and calling him "Monsieur le Merde." The dog stared straight ahead, paying no attention to him. Bennett pulled up on the opposite side of the raft. "Merlin, you're a cow killer," he sang out.

The dog flicked his eyes nervously to Bennett, then away.

I had an inspiration. This dog, though a little rough around the edges, was a survivor. He was also proud and dignified in his own quiet way. He reminded me of some cowboys I knew.

"I think we should call him 'Merle,'" I said. "That's a good, down-to-earth name."

At my voice, the dog sent me a glance, gauging my intentions. He held my eyes only a second before staring straight ahead. He seemed to know that chasing cattle wasn't going to win him friends. More than likely, he had either paid the price for it or had had a narrow escape. Dogs who chase cattle on Navajo lands are routinely shot. Maybe he had been creased by a bullet or perhaps someone had given him a second chance, letting him off with a sound beating. That could have been why he had flinched when I raised the stick. The dog now appeared to be waiting stoically for our reprimand, and perhaps that's why he had tried to appease me by licking my mouth.

"Merle," I said in a soft low voice. "Merle." He gave me another quick look, one brow up, the other down.

"Will that name work for you?"

The dog looked away, downriver, trying to ignore me. Then he began to tremble, not from his cold swim, but in fear.

*I*n central and southern Italy during the 1980s, about 800,000 free-ranging dogs lived around villages, among cattle, sheep, pigs, chickens, deer, boar, hare, other domestic dogs, and wild wolves. To estimate the impact these free-ranging dogs were having on livestock and wildlife, and particularly on the small, endangered wolf population, a team of biologists captured, radio-collared, and then observed one group of dogs in the Velino-Sirente Mountains of Abruzzo. The group consisted of nine adults—four males and five females—to whom forty pups were eventually born, only two surviving into adulthood, a testimony to the many dangers the free-ranging dogs faced as they eked out a livelihood. They were killed by people—primarily herders—as well as by foxes, wolves, and predatory birds.

Contrary to popular belief, the biologists discovered that the dogs didn't prey on wildlife or livestock. Instead, they scavenged at garbage dumps, as did most of the wolves. Since large groups of dogs prevented the smaller packs of wolves from feeding, the wolves sometimes went hungry. The researchers also noted that a small percentage of the dogs hunted deer and other wildlife, their prey varying by locale. In the Galápagos Islands, for instance, free-ranging dogs had been seen to prey on marine iguanas. On occasion, the Italian researchers added, such dogs were known to take down livestock, especially calves.

Among these dogs there were some individuals the researchers described as "stray" and others as "feral." The two are quite distinct. "Stray dogs," the scientists wrote, "maintain social bonds with humans, and when they do not have an obvious owner, they still look for one. Feral dogs live successfully without any contact with humans and their social bonds, if any, are with other dogs." Merle—for the name quickly stuck—was clearly a stray, and his previous experience with people had apparently left him both friendly and wary.

Stepping ashore that evening, he kept a low profile, still trying to gauge our reaction to his cow-chasing incident from a distance. Even when I filled his bowl with kibble, he studied me with caution. I slapped my hip and called, "Come on, chow's on." I rattled the bowl, put it down, clapped my hands, and extended them to his dinner.

His mistrust evaporated in an instant. Bounding forward, he devoured his food. When he was done, he let me rub his flanks. I put my face between his shoulder blades and blew a noisy breath into his fur. This made him wriggle in delight. Then I opened my lunch bag and cut him a piece of elk summer sausage. He plumped his bottom in the sand, whisking his tail back and forth as I handed him the tidbit. He took it from my fingers with care.

I knew that I was probably sending him a mixed message, since elk and cattle are both red meat. But if he and I stayed together, I reckoned we could sort this out in time.

During the next few days, he rode on the cooler and swam among the kayaks. He slept between us and sat around the stove, as polite and amiable a dog as one could wish for. The river became wilder, losing itself in deep canyons, and no more cattle appeared to tempt him. We also kept the latrine covered. Merle would follow us to it and sit a ways off, his expression turning wistful when the user of the latrine rose and closed its lid.

Once, after we climbed to an overlook high above the river, Benj, who is an avid herpetologist, caught a desert spiny lizard. I had seen Merle chase several jackrabbits—unsuccessfully—but when Benj offered him the ten-inch-long lizard, its tongue flicking in and out, to gauge his reaction, Merle backed up several paces, his eyes filled with worry. "That is a dangerous animal," they seemed to say, which was somewhat true—although desert spiny lizards eat mainly insects, and sometimes other lizards, they have powerful jaws that can inflict a nasty bite. Benj brought the lizard closer to him, but Merle would have nothing of it. He snorted several times, continuing to back up.

"Maybe he got bit by one," Benj said, "or just doesn't like reptiles."

A couple of days later, I saw Merle behave in a way that lent some credence to both of Benj's guesses. As Merle and I walked along a bench above the river our path joined that of a sidewinder rattlesnake, its trail curving through the sand. Merle took in a noseful of the spoor, lifted his head sharply, and studied the terrain ahead with concern.

"Snake," I said, trying to teach him the English word.

He glanced back at me, only the very tip of his tail moving, acknowledging what I had said. Then he took several steps to the side of the sidewinder's trail and walked parallel to it, keeping his eyes peeled.

On our way back to camp, we passed some coyote scat—two turds, each about four inches long and an inch in diameter. Merle's reaction to them was entirely different. He gave the coyote poop a sniff, then poked at the turds with his right paw, his nails taking them apart. He gave them another deep smell, like a wine connoisseur who has swirled his glass and is appreciating the wine's bouquet. His gaze became excited.

"*Coyoté,*" I said, giving the word its Spanish pronunciation.

He wagged his tail hard, cocked his leg, and squirted the coyote turds before enthusiastically scraping his hind legs over them. Puffing himself up, he trotted down the trail with his head swiveling dramatically from side to side, his entire body language announcing, "I will beat the living shit out of you if I find you."

His familiarity with the creatures of the desert impressed me; his burnished golden coat attracted me; his eyes wooed me. Yet for all the time we spent together, and despite sleeping by my side, Merle wasn't overt in his affections. He didn't put his head on anyone's lap; he didn't lick; he didn't offer his paw. Though still a pup, he was reserved and dignified. Life had taught him that trust needed to be earned.

On our last morning, as we came in sight of the muddy beach at Clay Hills and our waiting cars, which a shuttle company had driven down for us, I began to wonder whether this stray dog, with his mixture of fear and equanimity, would stick around or head off into the desert. I had once met a stray dog in Nepal whom I had thought was attached to me, but he had fooled me completely.

Like Merle, he simply appeared, walking into our camp in the remote Hunku Valley that lies beneath the great divide on which Mt. Everest looms. A young, black-and-brown Tibetan Mastiff, what Tibetans call a *Do Khyi,* he also had good manners and a highly evolved sense of how to feather his nest. He tagged along, eating our food and sleeping pressed to my sleeping bag, as my two companions and I trekked up the valley.

At the head of the valley, as we entered an icefall, the dog (whom we had named simply "the Khyi") went off to the left. Shortly he returned, sending us beseeching looks as he ran off again, trying to get us to follow him. We ignored him, keeping to our path, which we could see from the map was the direct route to the pass we had to climb. Many torturous hours later, we emerged from the icefall, only to find the Khyi, sitting there, waiting for us, an "I told you so" look on his face. Clearly, he had been this way before and knew a shortcut.

The next day we had to climb the Amphu Labtsa, a pass at the head of the valley that is the only way to exit the Hunku without retracing your steps. It's nineteen thousand feet above sea level, and to approach it you have to ascend increasingly steep snowfields, which the Khyi, still at our heels, navigated handily. However, when the last snowfield turned into a gully full of ice bulges, the Khyi was stopped short. We had fixed ropes for our four porters, and I brought up the rear, "jumaring" on the rope (using a mechanical device with teeth to assist in the ascent) and pushing the Khyi ahead of me, boosting him over the ice bulges.

At last, we came to a bulge too long and steep for the Khyi to surmount even with a push from me. He sat, unable to go up or down. Had he attempted to do either, he surely would have slipped and tumbled to his death. Like Merle, he was a four-eyed dog, with two tan patches on his black forehead, directly above his very brown eyes. He was unable to move them independently, as Merle could, yet, when furrowed, they gave him an expression of sobriety and command. Now, they seemed to say, "You know what we have to do."

I took off my pack and opened it wide. Since the ropes and ice-climbing gear were being employed on the mountain, I now had extra room. Lifting the Khyi by his armpits, I slipped him into the pack tail-first. He didn't protest in the least, and I continued up the ropes. He wasn't quite as big as Merle, maybe forty-five pounds. Still, given the other gear I was carrying, it meant I was toting about sixty-five pounds. Occasionally, the load pulled me off my stance, my crampons scraping across the ice as I swung on the rope.

The Khyi didn't stir. When I looked around, he met my eye and gave me a steady look, unfazed by the steep angle. Not once did he lick me.

At the top, we cramponed along the ridge crest, searching for an exit and discovering that we were at an impasse. The only negotiable descent was via a ledge whose far edge connected to a steep snowfield that in turn led to the glacier and valley far below. However, the ledge was about a hundred feet below us and we couldn't climb down to it, a fact that was brought home to us by one of the porters who, shifting his backpack nervously, dropped his sleeping bag. We watched it grow smaller and smaller as it tumbled several thousand feet through space until it hit the glacier.

The only way down, we could see, was to follow the sleeping bag's fall—a free rappel, with nothing beneath our feet but the dizzying drop. Since my friends had led up, I offered to lead down. When I swung off into space, aiming for the tiny ledge, the Khyi, immobile till then, gave a small whine. Braking myself on the rope, I turned and saw him peering down into the abyss, his eyes enormously wide. He glanced at me and whined again. He did not like the exposure.

When I reached the two-foot-wide ledge, I let him out of the pack, for he had begun to struggle. He ran several feet to the right, where the ledge ended, and a dozen feet to the left, where it merged into the steep snowfield on which it was obvious he'd get no purchase with his claws. He sat down, looking as if the wind had been knocked out of him, and stared to the distant valley. When the others arrived, he came over to me, sat by my pack, and let me put him in it. This was a dog without illusions.

We did two more rappels before the steep angle of the snowfield lessened. I took the Khyi from my pack, and without so much as a backward glance he ran off into the approaching night, his dark form vanishing on the glacier below.

Out of water, almost out of food, we camped in a sandy swale, glad to be down and looking forward to the morning, when we could cross the glacier and moraine in safety. When the sun rose, we found a trickle of ice melt, and as we sat drinking our tea who should come trotting up but the Khyi. He greeted each person briefly with his plume of waving tail, then came and sat before me. Looking me in the eyes, he raised his paw. I clasped him on the shoulder, and he put his paw on my arm in a comradely gesture. He stared into my eyes for a long moment, then whirled and disappeared among the ice.

I never saw him again, though a good friend of mine met him the next climbing season when the Khyi approached his camp only a few miles from where he had departed from us. He was convivial and well mannered, and attached himself to my friend's party, accompanying them to Island Peak's 20,300-foot-high summit.

Now, as we floated toward Clay Hills, I watched Merle sitting on the cooler and wondered whether he'd walk off into the desert to await the next group of river runners—like the Khyi, a canine adventurer and opportunist, a professional stray, a dog who liked scenic trips, his luminous eyes having said to how many others, "I am yours . . . for some elk sausage and a free ride."

We de-rigged the raft and loaded it in Benj's truck. We lashed down the kayaks, and Merle watched our every move with attention and without the least inclination to take off. We gathered in a circle, and he looked at us quizzically.

"What should we do with him?" I asked.

Pam had a little Husky named Kira and couldn't take on another dog. Bennett wasn't sure of his future. Benj lived and worked at the Teton Science School, where dogs weren't allowed, and Kim said a dog didn't fit into her lifestyle. I wondered whether a dog really fit into mine, and what I might do with him when I traveled on assignments. When I voiced this concern, Pam and Benj volunteered to dogsit.

Merle stared at me from under his crinkled brows. The thought of leaving him on this riverbank suddenly struck me as one of the great blunders I might make in my life.

"You want to become a Wyoming dog?" I asked him, thinking of how his back had felt against mine in the night and the expression on his face when he had realized that the howls echoing from the canyon walls were his own.

He gave his tail a slow, uncertain swish, having read the somewhat uneasy tenor of our discussion.

Our decision was delayed momentarily as Pam and Bennett, needing to be off, began a round of hugs with us. After they had driven off, Kim climbed into the truck, as did Benj. I held the door open for Merle. "Let's go. You're a Wyoming dog now—if you want."

A warm, sloppy grin spread across his face: "Me? You mean me?"

"Yep, I mean you," I said gently. "Come on, let's go home."

He bounded in, and settled himself behind the front seats on the floor.

An hour later, I turned around and said, "Hey, you guys, how you doing back there?"

Kim gave a thumbs-up, and Merle, who had fallen asleep, opened one eye and gave me a contented thump of his tail.

A Dog's
Agreement

by

H. Monro

Anyone who owns a Labrador retriever has probably heard the joke about who's taking who for a walk—dog or human? With your arm sore due to your Lab's strength, the joke's often not that funny.

This fun essay was first published in England's venerable comic institution, *Punch* magazine, and then reprinted in 1925's *Dog Stories from Punch*. It offers a dog's side of the joke.

*H*erewith, a dog's agreement, as imposed on a man, not his master, who offers to take him for a walk in the country:

1. Any attempt on your part to assume the attitude of a master will be regarded, for the purposes of this agreement, as an offence against the liberties of my species.

2. I will walk one hundred yards behind you, and, upon being called, I reserve the right to smile with my tail, and decline to decrease the distance. In view of the fact that you have the power to exhibit anger and other infirmities, you are to be considered, for the purposes of this walk, dangerous and, possibly, hostile.

3. I reserve the right, on the approach of a motor car, traction engine, or other vehicle, to stand directly in its path until my position has become appreciably perilous, and, on your calling me, to wag my tail to its full extent until such vehicle has passed. If necessary I shall be at liberty to dodge among the wheels. Any responsibility for my possible decease to remain entirely with you.

4. On the approach of a hostile dog the fight to ensue shall be conducted at your risk and at sufficient distance from you to obviate your intervention, and I am at liberty to receive such injuries as may render me an object of sympathy in the eyes of my Missus, and induce her to view the episode in the light of a delinquency on your part.

5. Any pause in the walk on your part shall be strictly observed by me, the interval of one hundred yards remaining undiminished. On your giving satisfactory evidence of an intention to retrace your steps homeward I have the right to turn about and precede you, increasing the distance between us so that I may arrive home at least a quarter-of-a-mile in front of you, with the full appearance of having been *lost*.

6. Upon your eventual return, I reserve the right to greet you, before my Missus, in a manner indicative of complete forgiveness. The injuries received on my casual adventures shall not prejudice the situation so far as I am concerned.

7. I reserve the right to accept in a spirit of tolerant fatigue any attempt on your part to put blame upon me.

8. In the event of your showing a disinclination to abide by any of the articles of this agreement I am entitled to exert such moral pressure on my Missus as may cause a temporary strain in your normal relation to each other, regard being always had, however, to your possible influence over her in the matter of my food.

9. None of the articles of this agreement shall prejudice such opportunities as may occur for making use of you for the purpose of future walks.

(Signed) Joggles

No blithe Irish lad was so happy as I;
No harp like my own could so cheerily play,
And wherever I went was my poor dog Tray.
—Thomas Campbell, *The Harper*

What's in a Name

by

Roger Welsch

Roger Welsch can best be described as a cross between Erma

Bombeck and Dr. Ruth—except he's male and lives in Nebraska with

his wife and several Labs.

Before turning his talents to canine psychology, Welsch was best

known as "the fat guy in overalls" on CBS TV's *Sunday Morning*,

where he offered up observations on rural and small-town life on the

plains. He's also the author of numerous books of fiction, folklore, and

humor, including 2006's *Forty Acres and a Fool: How to Live in the*

Country and Still keep Your Sanity.

This excerpt is taken from Welsch's memoir, *A Life with Dogs*,

published in 2004.

*M*an's respect for dogs is nothing new. The origins of our animal terms are often buried in ancient history. For example, the Romans called cows *bos,* and to this very day we call for our cows with that word. An ancient Germanic word *su* became our word "swine" and provides the shout we still use to call our hogs to slops— "sooEE!" What is the ultimate, climactic, most clichéd name for a dog in any cartoon or joke? "Fido." Of course. Fido. Again, it almost brings tears to my eyes when I remember that this most common of all dog names seems to bring it all together for us: Fido is Latin for "I am faithful." Isn't that perfect? Isn't that the motto of every dog that's ever lived? Aren't those precisely the words you read in your dog's eyes every time you look into them? "I am faithful." Ah, if only mankind could approach that kind of ideal!

People can be pretty unimaginative when naming their dogs, but my impression is that they put a good deal more thought, love, and creativity into naming their dogs than they do their children. Look at the lists of the most popular names for children these days. It's pretty obvious that modern parents are at least realistic about the prospects of their children amounting to anything important. I mean, jeez, you know for a fact that someone named Chelsey, Rusty, Heather, or Jamool is not destined to be President of the US of A!

I am always interested in what other people name their dogs: Pearl, Hillary, Fala, Him and Her, Harley, Priscilla, Freckles, Doowa, Odie, Buddy, Ricky Lee Anderson, Jr., Pearl, Chico, Patch, Jim, Yoni, Zeke, Emma, Elvis. I've always liked names like "Bill," "Joe," "Fred," and "Bob." I think giving a dog a plain ol' people name may be a trifle disrespectful to the dog, but it also says something about how the dog is seen as a peer, a human friend, even if maybe a little too good to be a human.

I think it is a terrific idea and tribute to name a dog "Fido"— "I am faithful"—or "Rex "or "King." One of these days I imagine I'll name a good black dog Fido, or maybe Blue.

"Spot" may seem a pedestrian name for a dog, but I have always wanted to name a black Lab retriever Spot. Wouldn't that lend the word a new import? I mean, you know, a 150-pound black Lab would be one really *big* spot. My next choice as a name for a black Lab is Snowball. My wife, Linda, does not have a flair for naming dogs; she named our golden retriever "Goldie." Uh-huh. Good. Golden retriever named Goldie. I reserve the right to name our real dogs, which is to say, our black Labs. At this point we have only two.

I believe that two is a subminimum number of black Labs anyone should have. Everyone should have one black Lab as the main dog, and then a codog for immediate assistance in welcoming the FedEx man, sniffing strange dog butts, cleaning out a food bowl, that kind of thing. You need a backup black dog in reserve behind those two so that if something should happen to your main dog and the codog moves up the hierarchy, you have your immediate replacement for the number two slot.

I would say those three dogs constitute your basic canine critical mass. Another two or three would provide a safety cushion that would certainly ease *my* mind and let me sleep more easily at night, but in our household the word has been let down that any more than two black dogs and there'll be one less helpmate woman. So, we have a rock-bottom base at this point of two black Labs. I have made few absolute proclamations in my life but one of them that I take very seriously is that life is too short to spend one single day without a black dog—so a second-string black dog is absolutely critical.

Our oldest black Lab is Thud. You'll hear a lot more about Thud as this book moves along. Thud is a bear of a dog (and at one time "Bear" was a name under consideration for him). "Thud," as we often note, is a name this big boy earned with his head. I don't believe it's a matter of clumsiness that causes him to bonk into things with such apparently contemptuous frequency. No, I prefer to believe that Thud simply doesn't care. Running into things with his head is for him a kind of signature behavior trait; moreover, I get the clear impression that Thud knows it amuses me when he runs into things with his head, so he just goes ahead and does it. He does whatever he thinks will please me. Thud is that way about things.

Our current codog is Abigail von der Pooper. The name "Abigail" came from my favorite brand of single-malt Scotch, Abelour, which is particularly and peculiarly feminine Scotch, much like Abigail herself. The name carries with it a certain sense of haughty royalty, even elegance, and she is that. The "von der Pooper" part is a result of her earliest demonstrated innate talent: Abbie is a half black Lab retriever, although, as my son, Chris, has pointed out, she is more of a "retainer" than a retriever. While she is willing to run after and seize whatever you throw to her, she is less enthusiastic about bringing it back or releasing it. And she is half Saint Bernard. But when we got her we had no idea that the half of her that is Saint Bernard would be the part that eats and poops.

Before Thud, we had Goldie and Lucky. As I noted before, Goldie was a golden retriever and without doubt the sweetest dog that ever lived . . . and perhaps one of the most devious. She was way too smart for her own good. Goldie had some delightful peculiarities about her. One of my favorites was that when I walked the dogs down to the river, she would walk calmly into the water to the depth of her neck (while the Labs ran insanely back and forth on the sandbars and plunged madly in and out of the water) and then . . . lie down. That left only her head, held as high as it would go, nose pointing straight up, out of the water. And she would just lie there, enjoying the water running over and around her. It was her joy: simple, quiet, calm.

There's an old joke about the dog that was so lazy he would wait for the neighbor's dogs to bark and then he would just nod. Goldie was like that, except instead of being lazy, she was smart. She'd go running up the outside stairs when anyone drove into our yard and bark twice, maybe three times. That would be enough to get everyone else barking, whereupon Goldie would retreat to a safer place under a cedar tree from where she could watch the action. She relaxed while the other dogs went nuts, us yelling at them to shut up, delivery people scrambling back into their vehicles seeking refuge, that kind of thing.

Contemporaneously with Goldie was Lucky. Lucky was a black Labrador retriever, and, man, was he ever a retriever! He *lived* to retrieve. Sticks, Frisbees, balls, ropes, whatever; it didn't make a whit of difference to Lucky what you threw, just as long as you were throwing. The most bewildering thing Lucky ever encountered in his life was someone who just sat there and wasn't throwing. He couldn't imagine a human being not throwing. A human being alive and not throwing made no sense whatsoever to him.

We got Lucky on a New Year's Day one year. I can't remember why we did that, but we did. I imagine it's because we knew somewhere in the back of our minds that if something evil happened to this new fuzzy black puppy, there'd be no veterinarian anywhere to help us. And of course that's what happened. There is a rule written down somewhere, maybe in the Bible, that when a dog gets hurt or sick it will always be late on a Friday or on a Saturday when your veterinarian is not in the office.

We never did figure out what happened to Lucky. One minute this new little fuzz-ball of a puppy was running around the yard with our other dog, Goldie, and the next minute he was spitting blood and having seizures. We guessed that maybe he fell off the patio retaining wall, or maybe Goldie accidentally stepped on him in the furor of welcoming him (Goldie would never have hurt a soul on purpose, even this annoying forcible insertion into her life). Whatever it was, he was mighty sick within hours of coming to us.

We finally found our vet and got the puppy to him, where the problem was diagnosed as way too serious for a small country clinic. Something was broken internally—bones, lungs—so we needed to get the new puppy to the nearest large city and find a vet with an X-ray unit. Many hours later, deep into the night, Linda and I were still sitting there, worried sick about this new little soul that was just clinging to life after only just arriving. We were crushed.

The recovery, both Lucky's and ours, was long and painful, and there were plenty of other problems along the way, too: falls, getting lost, nips from an overtaxed Goldie, cat slashes across a curious black nose. So when it came time to give the new Welsch a name, the choice seemed obvious. "Lucky" it was.

Before Goldie there was Blackjack, a huge bear of a Lab on whose flat head you could set two or three cans of beer, which he would have accepted with total equanimity. Blackjack was the first real black Labrador I ever owned. You won't be surprised to hear that Linda came up with this name. He (and Thud and Goldie) came "with papers." (So did Abbie and the rest of our dogs but the papers they came with were newspapers.)

Before Blackjack there was Slump, also black and sold to us as a Lab, but clearly *not* a Lab, a pinhead like hers only possible from Irish setter

blood. The name "Slump" came from a wonderful dog I saw in a James Garner film, and I tried to fit the dog into the name in this case rather than the much more reasonable and successful reverse. Slump was a nervous, crazy dog, not your typical black Labrador. I loved her nonetheless, probably in part because she was my first black dog. My buddy Mick was once doing some work on our house, looked at Slump, and then looked over the fence into the yard of an African-American neighbor of ours. He had a poodle. Mick wisely noted an important feature of the relationship between human beings and their dogs: "Why is that?" Mick asked rhetorically. "The white guy has a black dog . . . and the black guy has a white dog."

Slump was important to Linda and me because he was our first dog together. And my first dog after losing my previous dog in a fractious divorce. Jonathon Livingston Beagle, a.k.a. Fleagle, was as fine a dog as you can get by way of a nonblack dog. And a dog that was absolutely beyond reason. Fleagle simply refused to listen. He had his own ideas and he followed them without second thought. He did what he felt needed to be done. He might as well have been deaf. He wasn't at all belligerent about his defiance; he simply did not want you or anyone else to get the idea that he cared about what you wanted or were thinking. Nor did he have any regard for the works of man and God: fences, walls, doors, bogs, swamps, rivers, and distance meant nothing at all to Fleagle.

When I left my first wife, along with my home and all my belongings, not to mention my children and my dog, I lived in an apartment for a couple years and then a house about three miles away. As I recall, Fleagle traveled to my new digs a couple times in a car, but being a beagle he didn't get to see much of the trip since his eye level was well below the car window. But being a beagle, his eyes were pretty much an afterthought anyway; Fleagle lived by and followed his nose.

That's the only solution, at least, that I can imagine to the mystery that one morning I heard a scratching at my front door, opened it . . . and there was Fleagle. He was three miles from home, having traveled utterly unknown streets and neighborhoods, crossing several very busy, wide avenues. He didn't seem to think his trip was at all remarkable, but I was amazed. I fed him, watered him, greeted him heartily. I was a lonely, hurt man at the time, and Fleagle's grand dedication (the phrase "I am faithful" comes to mind) brought tears to my eyes. All I can figure is that he *smelled* his way through busy city streets from my old home to the new. Perhaps the hygiene of a new bachelor aided him in his quest.

How did Fleagle do it? Why didn't he get lost? How did he find my house? I penned him into my fenced backyard, figuring I'd drive him back home when I got home from work, but as I noted already Fleagle considered fences minor and momentary distractions. So by the time I returned from work, Fleagle was no longer in the yard. I called my former home and the children told me that they had in fact not even noticed that Fleagle had been gone, since he was now already back home, none the worse for wear, sound asleep on the front room couch.

Several more times during Fleagle's life in the city he got the whim to come visit me and he did. In yet another thoughtless and unwise decision, my erstwhile wife eventually exiled him to live with a farm family. A city-bred and -raised beagle on a farm. Yeah, that makes sense.

The first and only previous dog of that earlier marriage was, significantly, a nervous wreck of a dog we named Pooter in honor of her remarkable gastric reactions when eating leftover corn fritters. And because of the natural consequences that we very quickly realized and appreciated, we probably ate corn fritters more in our marriage and Pooter's tenure than any other single meal.

All dogs fart, I suppose, but some bring it off much better than others. Pooter wasn't much of anything else, but she was a sublime and industrial-grade farter. It wasn't simply that she farted more than most dogs (although she did) or that her products were audible (few dogs' are, despite braggarts' claims to the contrary) and otherwise notable (in an olfactory manner of speaking). No, the best part about Pooter's emissions was not so much the items themselves as her reaction to them. She could absolutely drive me into paroxysms of laughter because whenever she farted, she would haughtily jump up or to one side and look back at the offending place in the air where the bubble of stink now resided. . . *as if she had had nothing to do with it!* Other dogs I've known seem not to notice their social gaffes, although this may be a ruse to avoid the responsibility of the ecological damage they have wrought, but not Pooter. She was always the most offended by her own work and she made this disgust very clear.

She did ignore my glee, however.

In all my experiences with dogs, only Fleagle and Pooter were not with me until death did us part. My soul simply cannot stand discarding a dog. I find that a betrayal beyond any other. I mean that and, God knows, I've had plenty of the other kinds. I lost Fleagle in a divorce and then to a cold heart, so I guess I won't take responsibility for that treason, but Pooter . . . we gave Pooter away and I was a part of that conspiracy.

Pooter was with us for five years. We loved her even though she was a nasty, nervous, barky, bitey dog. It was just us—my wife, me, and Pooter—so her bitchy behavior (I am speaking here of Pooter's) was not a problem. But then along came our son, Chris. And then in rapid order, two daughters came. One daughter was adopted, so there were three infants introduced into our household within a little over two years. We feared this might be a problem for Pooter, and it was. It got to the point where we were worried about the welfare and safety of the children. We couldn't be angry with Pooter—she was there first, after all. And the children were obnoxious, startlingly loud, and stinky a lot of the time.

But it was obvious that something was going to have to be done, which is to say Pooter was going to have to go. Since she was nothing but a mutt, and a mutt with an evil disposition at that, and not at all a puppy, we knew it was not going to be easy to find her a new home. But since we couldn't bring ourselves to "put her to sleep," as the euphemism tends to go with pets, we started with what even we recognized as a vain effort to deal with her humanely—we put an ad in the paper.

Pooter wasn't like a used car whose faults could be concealed with sawdust in the transmission, a new paint job, and a dose of radiator sealant. Anyone who bothered to respond to our advertisement would eventually have to come to our house and meet this snarly little yapper. Her disposition simply could not be concealed.

Well, a little old lady telephoned in response to our posting, and I couldn't even try to promote Pooter as anything but what she was. I explained that she barked, yipped, nipped, and snarled every time anyone came to the door and there would be no way to stop her. We had tried and failed. To our astonishment, our caller absolutely giggled with glee; that was exactly what she wanted, she gushed, a little dog that would let her know when someone came to the door and give any visitor pause about coming in.

She drove immediately to our home and to our astonishment instantly fell in love with this most unlovable of dogs. And what's even more astonishing—miraculous, even— Pooter fell instantly in love with her. Pooter didn't go with her unwillingly. No, you could almost hear Pooter begging, "Gray-haired old lady, take me with you! Take me away from these loonies and their wretched children! I will yap and nip and bark at your pleasure! Let us spend the rest of our lives being nasty old snarlers together! Take me! Take me! Take me!"

They drove off and my wife and I sat there in our living room, surrounded by our squalling children, and we were amazed. And maybe just a little envious. Pooter had gotten off easy.

Now we're going to go back further in time to the brink of my tear-threshold, back to the first real love of my life, my first dog, the unfortunately named Toodles. I didn't name her Toodles. She came to me with that name. Sometimes that happens. I suppose one can call a dog anything one wants. People change their names after all and manage to deal with that. But I would feel, even to this day, terribly presumptuous doing that unless the dog changed the name his- or herself. Sometimes people name a pet and that name simply changes to fit the animal, just as Jonathan Livingston Beagle eventually (rather quickly, actually) became Fleagle. Our daughter Antonia was just four years old when she named our new farm kitty Love-Heart Love-Angel Love-Kitty; that ponderous moniker very quickly evolved to "Hairball." Toodles' name didn't do that. That's the name she came to us with and that's the name she kept. She seemed quite comfortable in fact with the name, so that was it.

I was home from school, maybe six years old, and I had the whooping cough. In those days when you got something like the measles, whooping cough, anything major, you were quarantined. No kidding, you had to stay at home and they put a big yellow sign on your front door warning people not to come in. Not only was I home sick from school, none of my friends could come visit me for weeks. It was a terrible isolation for a kid like me who normally ran the streets with his friends every day.

My family—Mom, Dad, some uncles and aunts—worked as domestics for the rich folks in town, sometimes as a first job, or in the case of my parents, as a second. Dad was a power engineer at the university powerhouse, but he also did lawn care for rich businessmen in town. Mom occasionally worked as a cleaning lady or cook for special occasions like parties at the same homes. My Aunt Edith was a live-in maid for a family of wealthy Jewish clothing store owners in Lincoln, Nebraska. Somewhere along the line Aunt Edith told these people. . . oh, what the heck. I'm going to tell you their names because they were such wonderful and generous people, and they are now gone, and I think they deserve credit for what they did next. Somewhere along the line Aunt Edith mentioned to Harry and Helen Simon that I was sick and lonely and would be for several weeks to come.

Now, the Simons were bright, well-educated people, and I can't help but think they must have known what they were doing when they offered to let my Aunt Edith bring their own beloved, new little puppy, a toy Boston terrier—their "Toodles" —to me to keep me company for a week or two. You don't lend a kid a dog for a week or two. Or an hour or two. You know what is going to happen. You're going to lose your dog. And the Simons did. I remember taking Toodles to my grandmother's house to return her to Aunt Edith when I was well so she could take Toodles back "home" to the Simons.

I thought I was going to die. I can still these 60 years later remember the anguish. My family is 100 percent German and not notably softhearted. We are disciplined people. Our kids don't get their way by crying. We do what needs to be done. And this borrowed dog needed to be returned. That was my father's absolute rule: Never borrow anything; but if you do, always return it in better condition than in which you received it. And here was his son, attempting not to return a loan at all! But I'm sure my obvious and utterly spontaneous pain—these were not the tears of a spoiled child! —must have been hard even for him to bear.

We returned home with Toodles and somehow, sometime, my folks must have talked with the Simons about what had happened. And the Simons let me keep their dog. Many years later I happened to encounter the Simons in a Lincoln restaurant and had a chance to thank them again for their incredible kindness. As if any thanks could ever be adequate to the gesture.

Toodles was my best friend all through my youth, from that point until my senior year in high school. When I walked home from elementary school, I always knew that when I rounded the corner at the bottom of the long hill at 12th and Lake Streets, I would instantly see a small black and white bundle of muscle launch itself from our front porch two blocks away and carry itself on scurrying legs all the way down to me, welcoming me back home.

I guess that's one of the reasons I love that old folk song "Old Blue." When Toodles died, she jarred the ground in my backyard for damn sure. I lost the best friend I'd had all my life. She was the only one who understood me through my adolescence. She was the very embodiment of love through my developmental years. It took me a long time to get over losing her; I never lost sight of her sense of dignity and devotion.

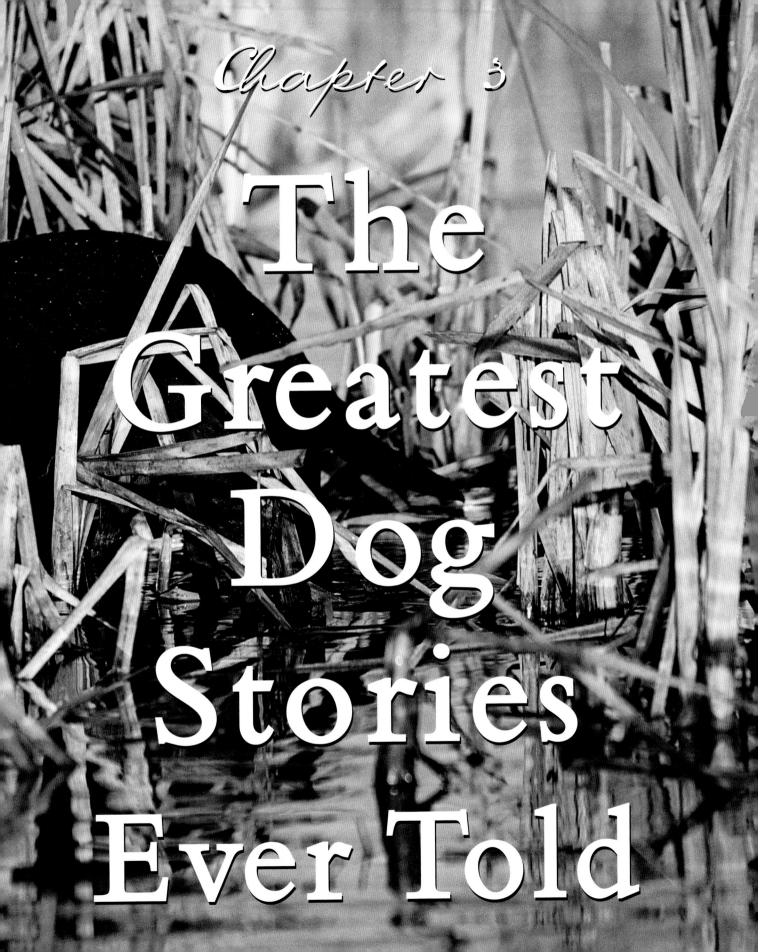

Chapter 3

The Greatest Dog Stories Ever Told

"Recollect that the Almighty, who gave the dog to be companion of our pleasures and our toils, hath invested him with a nature noble and incapable of deceit."
—Sir Walter Scott, *The Talisman*, 1825

Ben

by

Paul A. Curtis

Paul Curtis hunted with numerous canine companions during his long career as a shooting expert, editor, and author. Curtis served as the shooting editor for *Field & Stream* magazine for fifteen years and later as the editor of the magazines *Game* and *National Sportsman*. He contributed countless hunting sketches to the sporting magazines of his time, and penned seven books on hunting, including 1920's *Outdoorsman's Handbook*, 1927's *American Game Shooting*, and 1937's *The Highlander*.

"Ben," which originally appeared in Curtis' 1938 book, *Sportsmen All,* is the story of a multi-talented Lab from Scotland, memorable in the field not only to his owner but also to England's King George V.

A thick mist rolled in from the Atlantic. It swathed the Goat Fell, mighty sentinel of Bute, as in a winding sheet.

I knew before hearing my host's judgment, as we raided the mysterious dishes under their covers on the hot plate, that there would be no grouse shooting upon the high moors that day. His proposal, however, seemed quite as good indeed; and after a week's tramping in the heather above Glen Rosa and along Corrie Dhu, following such intrepid leaders of dogdom as Brodic Castle Brigadier, champion of Scotland and Ulster, it came as a relief. We were to try the low ground for a mixed bag, crossing Arran afoot, with a couple of gillies in attendance, aiming to reach a certain farmhouse in time for tea, where, afterwards, a good flight of wood pigeon was expected.

Thus we started, about ten o'clock. The motor swung out through the park drive, where the water dripped from the rank growth of rhododendron, past the Standing Stanes—rugged monoliths erected by the prehistoric people of the Isles long before the Roman Legions set foot on Scotia—on through the great iron gates, symbols of the dignity within, and purred along the narrow road which wandered like a white ribbon through the hills to the west, where the surge of the sea rolled relentlessly against Arran's rugged shores.

The motor slowed down at a quaint little bridge of the red stone of the country, and crooked as a dog's leg, so made in the old days that the devil might not cross, though why a gentleman so crooked and ingenious himself could not navigate them, has never been explained. On the other side of it the gillies rose from the heather and doffed their caps, wishing us a good morning in the soft Highland tone that is like a benediction, and received our lunch basket and shell bags.

There were but six of us: two gullies to carry the game and a plentiful supply of cartridges; Bonnie, an indefatigable red cocker that accompanied his master everywhere; a great lumbering brute of a Labrador; my host and me. We crossed a meadow, from which some lapwings rose lazily, conscious of their protection under the law, and assailed a steep bracken-clad slope into which Bonnie dove with industrious zeal.

In a moment one was sodden with moisture to the tails of his jacket, in evidence that whatever happened it would not be dry sport, but the action was swift. Before I had gone five rods there was a disturbance in the bracken, and a woodcock fluttered away in front of me, to go down at the

first crack. The great Labrador went after it on command and I watched him come floundering back through the low cover, head aloft, to disgorge the bird in the outstretched hand of the gillie. Meanwhile Bonnie pushed out a rabbit which fell to his master, and a moment later I rolled another down the hill. One does not mind a wetting midst such excitement.

Both Ben, the Labrador, and Bonnie were kept busy for the next two hours. Pushing through a grove of birches we bagged another cock, and at the report there was a sharp clatter of stiff wings, and some pigeons dashed from cover, of which we took our toll. A couple of hares were collected in the open, and sundry hedgerow rabbits, as well as a brace of black game from off the edge of the corn. Then we came to a stretch of bog, where the fun was fast and furious, for some snipe were there; we accounted for several couple, at the expenditure of considerable ammunition, before we capped the morning with a brace of teal at the far end. Such is rough shooting on Arran.

Through all this I had time to develop an increasing admiration for big Ben—floundering up to his belly in the black bog where the snipe rose—retrieving hares and sundry rabbits, to say nothing of the teal and the black game. He had done nobly and with never a mistake. Staunch as a rock he stood at heel behind the gillie, until sent out with a wave of the hand and a soft word of command to do his stuff, picking up his quarry and coming promptly back with head and stern in the air, always at a gallop. Plainly Ben was a lucky dog, for he was doing the thing which he loved best.

As the sun came out it revealed a broad stretch of purple moor low on the edge of the sea. My host suggested that we work it, to add a few brace of grouse to the variegated bag, while our sodden garments dried upon us, before sitting down to a belated lunch. Some tourists cycling by on the shore road paused to watch the sport and we soon gave them action, as a large covey rose with a cackle of protest and winged it back to the mountains where they belonged. We took eight-and-a-half brace off that bit of moor before we reached our resting place beside a little monument which had been erected to commemorate the day when King Edward VII had lunched there on a similar shoot with the father of my host.

Whilst we took off our shoes and wrung the water from our stockings, the gillies dumped their game bags on the ground and their contents were laid out in orderly array. Thirty-six head we had, according to my game register, and the afternoon flight yet to come. When the lads had put it away again and, spreading out the lunch, had retired to the lee of a boulder to eat their own, the two dogs sat down to watch us, with slavering interest, from an orderly distance.

I quaffed a bracer from a horn cup, diluted with burn water, and waded into one of the most delicious dishes in the world—a cold grouse pie. Having appeased my appetite I looked up, and there was the polite Ben gazing at me with a pleading look in his dark eyes, while his huge maw of a mouth slobbered and drooled like a cataract. Really, it was too much to bear! I reached into the pie and picked out a toothsome bit, as he cocked his head on one side, tail awag in anticipation. Having deftly caught the offering, with a smack of the chops he sat back again on his haunches, eying his master furtively, in fear of a reprimand.

"A grand retriever that—and well behaved too," I observed.

"Yes," said His Grace, "he is well broken. Ben is probably the best one I have ever had, but nevertheless he caused me one of the most embarrassing moments of my life. Perhaps his good behavior is an atonement, but I shall never live it down."

"What happened?" I asked, knowing from the twinkle in his eye as he smiled reminiscently at Ben, that behind it there was a story worth hearing. He crossed one brawny knee over the other and settled himself in the heather before he replied. The thin cry of a curlew came to us from the rim of the sea. My eyes rested on the soft blue of the water, where far out on the edge of nowhere the little dun sails of the herring fleet were visible. Beyond them again lay Ireland, but the haze was too thick to reveal it. Loading my briar, I waited in anticipation.

"We used to have a place in the Midlands where we spent the winter. We went there to escape the rigors of that season in Scotland, and while I shot, the family hunted with the local packs. There was good partridge and pheasant shooting in that country. One of my neighbors had a magnificent

pheasant shoot, and once, some years ago, King George came to shoot with him. The owner had been to no end of trouble to provide the best of sport and when I was invited, naturally I accepted, and I took Ben, who was then a highly promising three-year-old, with me.

"We drew for position, which His Majesty always insisted upon, and it so happened that I was next to him in the first drive. As you know, His Majesty was a first-class shot—one of the best in the Empire—and absolutely deadly on high pheasants, but aside from that keepers have canny ways of their own of pushing the birds to that part of the line where they know from previous experience, the best guns will be. Naturally they want to have a big bag and one cannot prevent their doing it or blame them especially. So, despite the fact that there had been no favoritism, and he had drawn his peg with the rest of us for position, there was always an exceptional showing of birds over that part of the line where the King was posted, and, naturally, he had a lot of them about him when the whistle blew.

"Our friend Ben, over there, behaved splendidly, sitting behind my loader like a graven image until the drive was over, and retrieving my birds with dashing style, just as he did today. I was proud of him and confident in his behavior, so when he had collected my lot, I called him to heel and went over to the King's stand.

"'Sir,' I said, 'may I send out my dog to assist?'

"'Ah, thanks very much, Montrose,' he replied. 'Very kind of you.' So, as I said, full of confidence, I sent Ben out again and he behaved quite up to form, earning an approving comment from His Majesty.

"Well, to make a long story short, after lunch in the rotation of the stands I found myself again beside His Majesty, and we had a furious drive. The birds were coming over so high against a grey sky that they looked like sparrows, but time and again I observed that he had two dead in the air in front of him as he reached for his second gun. When the beaters came through to the edge of the woods and the feu de joie was over, Ben made my pick-up and I again joined the King.

"'By jove, we have need for him this time,' he said, or words to that effect, and his eyes were sparkling. He had as many birds grassed behind him as he had in front, and Ben and his Clumbers were sent out further and further, bringing in the nearest first and then extending their range.

"It was a double drive, in which the guns remained in the same stands while the beaters went around and drove the birds back from the opposite direction, together with the undisturbed ones which occupied the woods, which became our new front. Under such conditions I made a mistake in sending Ben out so far, as he might easily have put back some birds near the edge, but he was doing splendidly until a winged bird, lying doggo in a clump of grass, got up in front of him and legged it for the cover, with the brute in hot pursuit. I blew my whistle like mad, but he disappeared in the woods—and then it happened!

"I heard him giving tongue frantically, while keepers cursed and shouted, and, to our utter amazement, hares broke from the woods in every direction, the majority of them dashing across our front, with that silly brute coursing as if he were in the Waterloo Cup, as he passed the King.

"Of course we were all disorganized—no one had a gun loaded— most of us, having finished the pick-up, were walking about smoking cigarettes with some neighbor when the Charge of the Light Brigade went through our batteries. There were a few scattered shots into the rear guard that bowled over a couple, but almost everyone, save myself, was too paralyzed with laughter even to lift a gun."

His Grace paused reminiscently before he continued with a hint of reproach in his voice. "You know, my host was furious with me! Oh, quite!—in fact he never asked me over again—would hardly speak to me. It seemed that there were a lot of hares on his place and the head keeper had them driven into that woods the day before. Nets had been drawn about it with a lot of roots in the center to hold them. When the hares had been pushed in the opening, the nets were quietly closed, and there they were. It was hoped that it would provide a surprising diversion on the last drive and would have, too, if Ben had not landed in the middle of them just as the net was opened. I never really blamed him, poor chap; such a collection of hares scattering about like a bomb shell would be enough to put anyone off. Of course I never heard the end of it—hardly dared go near my club for a month.

"About a year later I was aboard the Admiral's flagship at Portsmouth when His Majesty reviewed the Fleet. We senior officers were drawn up on the quarter-deck when he was piped aboard. He walked slowly down the line, shaking hands with everyone, passed me with a word of recognition, and then bethought himself and turned back. With a gleam of amusement in his eyes he raised himself on his toes, with a hand cupped to his lips, and whispered into my ear, 'Oh, I say, Montrose, how *is* Ben?'"

When we reached the designated farm some hours later and had disposed of a formidable tea, which the farmer's wife had awaiting us, the light was already soft on the hills. Hurriedly we made off to a fine stand of firs surrounded by fields of yellowing corn, where the wary wood pigeons were expected to come to roost. As the gillies were going off to expedite matters by putting them up from nearby covers, I was placed at my stand with Ben for a companion. I was cautioned to let the birds come well in so that they would not drop in the corn, and if any did, on no account to let that lumbering brute go after them, as he would trample it down like a hippopotamus in a rice paddy. Ben sat down patiently beside me, as I loaded, and we prepared to wait.

The little world about us was busy in its quiet way, preparing for the night. Sheep bleated on the near-by hills, and from the slobs offshore the curlews were beginning to flight inland with plaintive cries, while their smaller brethren of the coast hustled complainingly about, gleaning the last bit of provender before the encroaching tide.

Silently a pigeon swept in overhead, and, spying us, swiftly changed direction with a diverting dive, but not too late to be intercepted. Ben retrieved it and I cleared his mouth of the feathers. There were several lots of pigeons now in the air, winging about at long range, as the walkers put them up. I shot a couple and missed as many more. Then came a lull. From somewhere nearby we heard the mellow COO-COO-COO of a bird that had slipped into the trees from in back, unaware of our presence, and Ben cocked his ears, while from a wee shealing on the brae above us came the soft strains of a lament, as some shepherd practiced upon his pipes. Then, on a sudden clatter of wings that roused us from daydreams, a

flight of pigeons was all about us, and for a few moments I was busy loading and firing. There was a constant flow of birds towards the woods, and the more distant ones were not disturbed by the firing. When it was over I had several of them scattered about me, which Ben found with ease, but there were a few more out in the corn—where they had inadvertently fallen— and he knew it too. Ben started for it and with a vision of the irate farmer and my instructions, I called him back.

"No! Ben—aboo!"

Like a flash he put on the brakes and came back to heel. There was no doubt about it— that day when he ran amuck and mussed up the King's hare drive—Ben had been taught a never-to-be-forgotten lesson.

Ike: A Good Friend

by

Gary Paulsen

Gary Paulsen is a prolific writer—and prolific lover of dogs. Over the
years, he worked as a trapper, migrant farm worker, and singer, but
eventually found his true calling as an author. He has penned more than
eighty books, including a series of adventure stories for young readers,
such classics as *Hatchet*.

In 1998, Gary compiled his reminiscences of his favorite dogs into
the memoir *My Life in Dog Years*, a glowing tribute to his canine friends.
As he writes in his introduction, "I have always had dogs and will have
dogs until I die. I have rescued dozens of dogs from pounds; always have
five or six of them around me, and cannot imagine living without dogs.
They are wonderful and, I think, mandatory for decent human life. All
that said, there are some dogs that are different, special in amazing ways."

"Ike: A Good Friend" is one of these. At its most basic, this a
hunting story. But in truth it's much, much more.

*M*uch of my childhood I was alone. Family troubles—my parents were drunks—combined with a devastating shyness and a complete lack of social skills to ensure a life of solitude. This isolation was not natural, of course, especially for a child, and most of the time I was excruciatingly lonely. I sought friends whenever I could, but was rarely successful.

When I was very young these times of aloneness were spent making model airplanes, reading comic books or just daydreaming. But when I was twelve, living in a small town named Twin Forks in northern Minnesota, an uncle gave me a Remington .22 rifle he'd bought at a hardware store for ten dollars. I ran to the woods.

It is not somehow "politically correct" to hunt, and that is a shame for young boys. For me it was not only the opening into a world of wonder, it was salvation. I lived and breathed to hunt, to fish.

Two rivers ran out of town, one to the north and one to the east, and any day, hour or few minutes I could spare I would run these rivers. The first year I hunted mostly rabbits and ruffed grouse—feeding myself in the process. I scuffled along in old boots with a box of .22 long rifle cartridges in my pocket and the single-shot rifle in my hand. On my back was an old army surplus light pack I'd bought with money from setting pins at the local bowling alley. In the pack I had matches, usually a loaf of bread, salt and an old aluminum pot for boiling water.

There was great beauty in running the rivers, especially in the fall when the leaves were turning. The maples were red gold and filtered the sunlight so that you could almost taste the richness of the light, and before long I added a surplus army blanket, rolled up over the pack, and I would spend the nights out as well. During school—where I did badly—I would hunt in the evenings. But on Friday I was gone, and I would frequently spend the entire weekend alone in the woods.

The problem was that I was alone. I had not learned then to love solitude—as I do now—and the feeling of loneliness was visceral, palpable. I would see something beautiful—the sun through the leaves, a deer moving through the dappled light, the explosion of a grouse flying up through the leaves—and I would turn to point it out to somebody, turn to say, "Look . . ." and there would be no one there.

The second fall after I'd started living in and off the woods I decided to hunt ducks. Miles to the north were the great swamps and breeding grounds of literally millions of ducks and geese, and when the migratory flights started south the sky would seem to darken with them. The .22 rifle was not suited for ducks—was indeed illegal for them—so I saved my money setting pins and bought an old single-shot Browning twelve-gauge shotgun from a kid named Sonny. The gun had a long barrel and a full choke, and with number four shot seemed to reach out forever. I never became really good with it, but could hit now and then when the ducks were flying at the right angle. Duck hunting soon became my life.

I did not have decoys but I made some blinds six miles out of town where there were cattail swamps. I would walk out there in the dark, leaving the house at three in the morning, nestle into the blinds and wait for the morning flights to come in from the north. Usually I would get one or two ducks—once a goose—but some I wounded or didn't kill cleanly and they would get into the swamp grass and weeds in the water and I couldn't find them.

It was about then that I met Ike.

Ike was a great barrel-chested black Labrador that became one of the best friends I've ever had and was in all ways an equal; not a pet, not something to master, but an equal.

I had had other dogs. Snowball in the Philippines, then a cocker spaniel somebody gave me named Trina. They were sweet and dear and gave love the way only dogs can, with total acceptance, but Ike was the first dog I'd ever known not as a pet but as a separate entity and partner. We met strangely enough. It was duck season and I was going hunting. I woke up at three and sneaked from the basement, where I stayed when my parents were drunk—which was all the time—up into the kitchen. Quietly I made two fried egg sandwiches at the stove. I wrapped them in cellophane (this was well before sandwich bags), folded them into a paper sack and put them in my pack along with a Thermos of hot coffee. Then I got my shotgun from the basement. I dumped a box of shells into the pockets of the old canvas coat I'd found in a trunk in the back of the coal room. I put on the knee-high rubber boots I'd bought at army surplus.

I walked from the apartment building four blocks to the railroad, crossed the tracks near the roundhouse yard, crossed the Eighth Street bridge and then dropped down to the riverbank and started walking along the water.

The river quickly left settled country and headed into woods, and in the dark—there was just the faintest touch of gray on the horizon— it was hard going. The brush pulled at my clothes and after a mile and a half the swamps became more prevalent so that I was wading in muck. I went to pull myself up the bank and walk where the ground was harder.

It had been raining, mixed with snow, and the mud on the bank was as slick as grease. I fell once in the darkness, got to my feet and scrabbled up the bank again, shotgun in one hand and grabbing at roots and shrubs with the other. I had just gained the top, brought my head up over the edge, when a part of the darkness detached itself, leaned close to my face and went:

"Woof."

It was that distinct—not "arf" nor "ruff," nor a growl, but the very defined sound of "woof." I was so startled that I froze, mouth half open. Then I let go of the shrub and fell back down the mud incline. On the way down the thought hit me—bear. Something big and black, that sound—it had to be a bear. Then the word gun. I had a gun. I landed on my back and aimed up the bank, pulled the hammer back and put my finger on the trigger before I realized the gun wasn't loaded yet. I never loaded it while walking in the dark. I clawed at my pockets for shells, found one, broke open the gun and inserted a shell, slammed it shut and was going to aim again when something about the shape stopped me. (It was well it did—I had accidentally jammed the barrel of the shotgun full of mud when I fell. Had I pulled the trigger the shell would have blown up in my face.)

There was just enough of the dawn to show a silhouette. Whatever it was remained at the top of the bank. It was sitting there looking down at me and was the wrong shape and size for a bear. It was a big dog, a black dog. But it was a dog and it wasn't attacking.

I lowered the gun and wiped the mud out of my eyes, stood and scraped mud off my clothes. I was furious, but not at the dog. There were other hunters who worked the river during duck season and some of them had dogs. I assumed that one of them was nearby and had let his animal run loose, scaring about ten years off my life.

"Who owns you?" I asked the shape. It didn't move or make any further sounds and I climbed the bank again and it moved back a few feet, then sat again.

"Hello!" I called into the woods around me. "I have your dog here!"
There was nobody.

"So you're a stray?" There were many stray dogs in town and some of them ran to the woods. It was bad when they did because they often formed packs and did terrible damage. In packs they were worse than wolves because they did not fear men the way wolves did and they tore livestock and some people to pieces.

But strays were shy and usually starved. This dog stayed near me and in the gathering light I could see that he was a Labrador and that he was well fed. His coat was thick and he had fat on his back and sides.

"Well," I said. "What do I do with you?"

This time his tail thumped twice and he pointedly looked at the gun, then back at my face, then down the side of the river to the water.

"You want to hunt?"

There, he knew that word. His tail hammered his sides and he stood, wiggling, and moved off along the river ahead of me.

I had never hunted with a dog before and did not know for certain what was expected of me. But I started to follow, thinking we might jump up a mallard or teal. Then I remembered my fall and the mud and that the gun was still loaded. I unloaded it and checked the bore and found the end packed with mud. It took me a minute to clean it out and reload it and before I'd finished he'd come back and sat four feet away, watching me quietly.

It was light enough now for me to see that he had a collar and a tag so he wasn't a stray. It must be some town dog, I thought, that had followed me. I held out my hand. "Come here."

But he remained at a distance and when it was obvious that I was ready to go he set off again. It was light enough now to shoot—light enough to see the front bead of the shotgun and a duck against the sky—so I kept the gun ready and we had not gone fifty yards when two mallards exploded out of some thick grass near the bank about twenty yards away and started up and across the river.

It was a classic shot. Mallards flying straight up to gain altitude before making off, backlit against a cold, cloudy October sky. I raised the gun, cocked it, aimed just above the right-hand duck to lead his flight and squeezed the trigger.

There was a crash and the recoil slammed me back. I was small and the gun was big and I usually had a bruise after firing it more than once. But my aim was good and the right-hand duck seemed to break in the air, crumpled and fell into the water. I had shot ducks over the river before and the way to get them was to wait until the current brought the body to shore. Sometimes it took most of the morning, waiting for the slow-moving water to bring them in.

This time was different. With the smell of powder still in the air, almost before the duck finished falling, the dog was off the bank in a great leap, hit the water swimming, his shoulders pumping as he churned the surface and made a straight line to the dead duck. He took it in his mouth gently, turned and swam back, climbed the bank and put the duck by my right foot, then moved off a couple of feet and sat, looking at me.

I made sure the duck was dead, then picked it up and tied it to my belt with a string I carried for the purpose. The dog sat and watched me the whole time, waiting. It was fully light now and I moved to him, petted him—he let me but in a reserved way—and pulled his tag to the side so I could read it. *My name is Ike.* That's all it said. No address, no owner's name, just one short sentence.

"Well, Ike"—at this his tail wagged—"I'd like to thank you for bringing me the duck . . ."

And that was how it started, how I came to know Ike.

Duck season soon consumed me and I spent every morning walking and hunting the river. On school days I would go out and come back just in time to get to classes and on the weekends I stayed out.

And every morning Ike was there. I'd come across the bridge, start down the river, and he'd be there, waiting. After a few mornings he'd let me pet him—I think he did it for me more than him—and by the end of the first week I was looking forward to seeing him. By the middle of the second week I felt as if we'd been hunting with each other forever.

And he knew hunting. Clearly somebody had trained him well. He moved quietly, sat in the blind with me without moving, watched the barrel of the gun to see which duck I was going to shoot at, and when I shot he would leap into the water. On those occasions when I missed—I think more often than not—he would watch the duck fly away, turn to me and give me a look of such uncompromising pity and scorn that I would feel compelled to apologize and make excuses.

"The wind moved the barrel," or "A drop of water hit my eye when I shot." Of course, he did not believe me but would turn back, sitting there waiting for the next shot so I could absolve myself.

When the hunting was done he'd walk back with me to town, trotting alongside, until we arrived at the bridge. There he would stop and sit down and nothing I did would make him come farther. I tried waiting him out to see where he would go but when it was obvious that I wasn't going to leave he merely lay down and went to sleep, or turned and started back into the woods, looking back to see if we were going hunting again.

Once I left him, crossed the bridge and then hid in back of a building and watched. He stayed until I was out of sight and then turned and trotted north away from the bridge along the river. There were no houses in that direction, at least on the far side of the river, and I watched him until he disappeared into the woods. I was no wiser than I had been.

The rest of his life was a mystery and would remain so for thirty years. But when we were together we became fast friends, at least on my part.

I would cook an extra egg sandwich for Ike and when the flights weren't coming we would "talk." That is to say, I would talk, tell him all my troubles, and he would sit, his enormous head sometimes resting on my knee, his huge brown eyes looking up at me while I petted him and rattled on.

On the weekends when I stayed out, I would construct a lean-to and make a fire, and he would curl up on the edge of my blanket. Many mornings I would awaken to find him under the frost-covered blanket with me, sound asleep, my arm thrown over him, his breath rumbling against my side.

It seemed like there'd always been an Ike in my life and then one morning he wasn't there and I never saw him again. I tried to find him. I would wait for him in the mornings by the bridge, but he never showed again. I thought he might have gotten hit by a car, or his owners moved away. I mourned him and missed him. But I did not learn what happened to him for thirty years.

I grew and went into the crazy parts of life, army and those other mistakes a young man could make. I grew older and got back into dogs, this time sled dogs, and ran the Iditarod race across Alaska. After my first run I came back to Minnesota with slides of the race to show to all the people who had supported me. A sporting goods store had been one of my sponsors and I gave a public slide show of the race one evening.

There was an older man sitting in a wheelchair and I saw that when I told a story of how Cookie, my lead dog, had saved my life his eyes teared up and he nodded quietly. When the event was over he wheeled up to me and shook my hand.

"I had a dog like your Cookie—a dog that saved my life."

"Oh—did you run sleds?"

He shook his head. "No. Not like that. I lived up in Twin Forks when I was young and was drafted to serve in the Korean War. I had a Labrador that I raised and hunted with, and left him when I went away. I was gone just under a year; I got wounded and lost the use of my legs. When I came back from the hospital he was waiting there and he spent the rest of his life by my side. I would have gone crazy without him. I'd sit for hours and talk to him and he would listen quietly . . . it was so sad. He loved to hunt and I never hunted again." He faded off and his eyes were moist again. "I still miss him . . ."

I looked at him, then out the window of the sporting goods store. It was spring and the snow was melting outside but I was seeing fall and a boy and a Lab sitting in a duck blind. Twin Forks, he'd said—and the Korean War. The time was right, and the place, and the dog.

"Your dog," I said. "Was he named Ike?"

He smiled and nodded. "Why, yes—but how . . . did you know him?"

There was a soft spring rain starting and the window misted with it. That was why Ike had not come back. He had another job.

"Yes," I said, turning to him. "He was my friend . . . ."

Dog
v.
Postman

by

R. Magill

Labrador retrievers and postal workers have an established and long-running relationship. The question remains, though, why do postal employees in particular seem to garner such grandiose attention from our dogs?

This fun essay first appeared in a British comic magazine, *Punch*, and was reprinted in 1925's *Dog Stories from Punch*.

*B*etween dogs and postmen there exists an antipathy which makes the Wars of the Roses look as harmless as a Primrose League conversation. Now there are dogs who appreciate the finer points of a burglar's character; there are others who are prepared to concede a certain amount of self-determination to cats; there are those who will even allow a policeman to become familiar; but no self-respecting dog has ever yet met a postman without endeavouring to annihilate him, boots, badge, fore-and-aft hat and notebook too. No sooner does the faithful hound in the kennel hear the double rat-tat of the emissary of the P.M.G. [Post Office] than he proceeds to asphyxiate himself in an attempt to relieve the unemployment problem by creating a vacancy for an able-bodied man who can deliver letters and run well.

Many scientists have tried to explain this phenomenon. It was thought at one time to be a political matter. Dogs are instinctively Conservative, as everybody knows who has suggested nationalising any dog's accumulated wealth of bones. Postmen, on the other hand, are more probably either Radical or Labour. But one does not bite one's political opponents. Rather one prays for them.

Another suggestion was that in remote ages some ancestor of the postman must have played the ancestor of the dog a dirty trick; but this appears as a fallacy when you consider that toy-dogs, whose ancestors could not possibly have been dogs, hate postmen. Even the Papillon, which seems to be the result of a mis-alliance between a mouse and a mosquito, barks its defiance of postmen through the medium of a megaphone introduced to obviate the risk of a broken blood-vessel.

The real reason for the feud is that the dog is in the main an intelligent animal. He watches the effect of the morning's post. His beloved master grows angrier and angrier as he reads. Seventy-five percent of his correspondence consists of accounts rendered, appeals from some charitable institution or offers from some grand old English gentleman to lend him five to five million pounds on his note of hand alone. At the end his master disagrees with his mistress, snaps at the servants and, if there should happen to be a reminder about the dog-licence amongst his letters, he may even kick the dog.

Who is it that brings these letters? Unquestionably the postman. Therefore the dog does his best to protect the home against these destroyers of domestic peace.

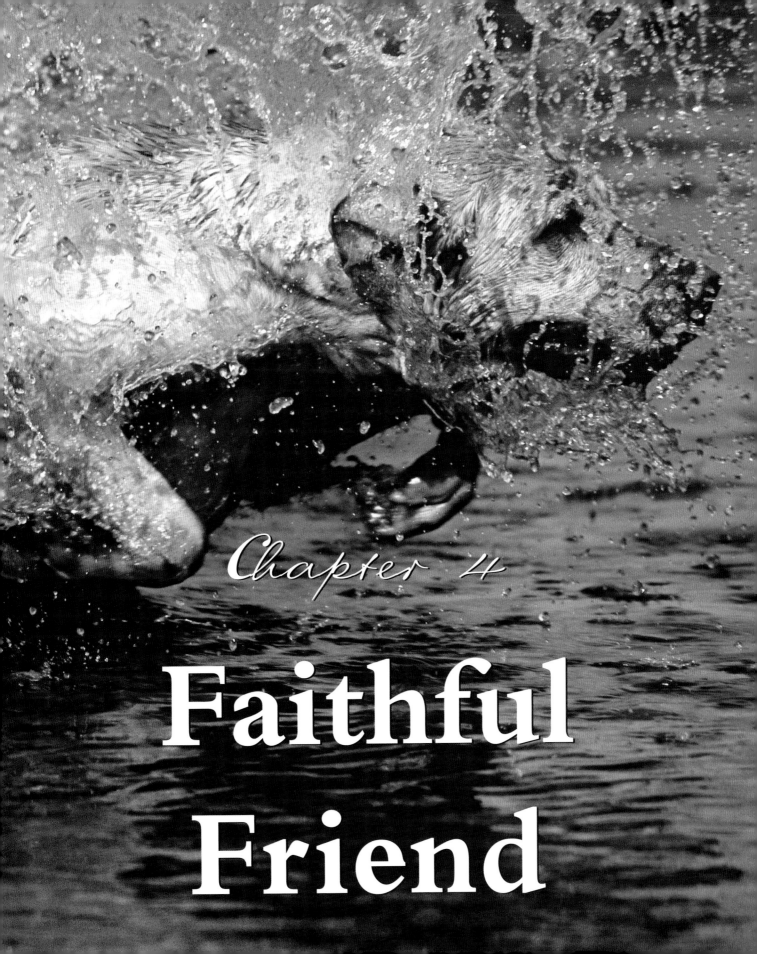

Chapter 4

Faithful
Friend

"The great pleasure of a dog is that you may make a fool of yourself with him and not only will he not scold you, but he will make a fool of himself too."
—Samuel Butler

Samson's Strength

by

Carol Davis

Carol Davis has been a newspaper and magazine editor for some twenty years, writing about all aspects of life. And throughout that time, she has shared her own life with dogs, including Frosty, Tramp, Beau, Brandy, Bubba, Toby, Maggie, Buddy, Spencer, Sam, and Abby.

Davis is also the author of 2007's homage *Farm Dogs: A Celebration of the Farm's Hardest Worker*.

In this essay, she writes of her Labrador, Samson, and his big heart.

The sound of Maggie, my Lab mix, barking furiously, signaled something was wrong one spring morning about four years ago. She had several barks: one meant, "Hurry up with my dinner;" one indicated that someone had driven up; and one meant, "Snake! Snake!"

This bark sounded perilously close to her snake bark.

A glance outside revealed that she wasn't snapping and hopping around a wayward reptile. Her fury and fear was directed at some kind of animal intruder—a raccoon, possum, or unfamiliar dog—under the porch at the house across the road and she was aggressively trying to run him off.

Later, this intruder moved from under the porch to those neighbors' front stoop, and I could see that it was a dog. They must have gotten a new pet. I knew that Maggie, who had lost interest in protecting her turf, eventually would befriend this newcomer; she would just have to get familiar with him.

Working at home as a freelance writer, with a desk that looked out a large front window, I could see my neighbors' comings and goings, despite the fact that our house sits way back off the country road. So I took notice when, for several days, they would drive up, ignore the dog and walk into the house. That was odd. Why would you bring a new pet home and then ignore it?

Shortly after, I met up with a member of that family by our mailboxes, and asked if they had gotten a new dog.

"No," she replied. "He just showed up one day and won't leave. We don't know where he came from. We're not feeding him, so we hope he'll go away."

She walked back down her driveway as I stood there, saddened, and a bit angry, by what she said. How could you not feed a hungry animal? I glanced at the dog, who hadn't budged from the front stoop for days. He returned my gaze.

With the realization that someone finally was acknowledging him, he stood up and hesitantly inched his way across the neighbor's yard toward me, with his head down, tail tucked between his legs and eyes that seemed to say, "Please don't hurt me." His ribs also had begun to show.

As he moved closer, responding to my gentle encouragement, I realized that he was a Lab, my favorite kind of dog. I also noticed that the top of his brown head appeared to have something—oil perhaps?—all over it. As he came closer, I realized with horror what it was: blood. His scalp had been laid open and, of course, had remained untreated.

That did it. "Come on, boy," I said, and turned down the gravel driveway. The Lab's eyes perked up instantly and he eagerly followed. "At last, a friendly person," he seemed to think. And despite an injured, infected head and empty belly, this homeless dog wagged his tail. Wagged his tail! I knew then that he was something special.

Maggie, meanwhile, was beside herself that this intruder was actually in her yard, and I put her inside so I could tend to him.

The first priority was to get some food in his stomach and to treat his head wound. But I had to be careful in handling him; he seemed friendly, but I didn't know his disposition, and an injured or scared animal can be dangerous.

My solution: do both simultaneously. So, I got a dish and filled it with dog food and while this poor foundling ate ravenously, I sprinkled an antiseptic powder that had been recommended by my old country veterinarian years before. This amazing antiseptic foot powder for humans was available only in old-time pharmacies and, over the years, had quickly healed my dogs and cats whenever they got into scrapes—some serious—with other animals. I knew this would heal this poor stray's wound—at least on the outside.

So, that would be our routine for the next week or so: he was fed in the morning and evening at first, and as he gratefully gobbled his food, I powdered his head, unbeknownst to him, with antiseptic. And he began to heal.

A visit to the vet determined that the stray, now named Samson—nicknamed Sam or Sammy—was about 1½ years old. He got his shots, neutered, and wormed, because we didn't want him passing any parasites on to Maggie.

Maggie, meanwhile, had come to accept him, too. After all, who could resist this dog? His loving nature was apparent immediately after coming to live with us, and he easily responded to the caring attention he was getting. He played tug-of-war and tag and chase with Maggie. He lived to retrieve his new ball. And he was always, always happy to see you. You could see it in his eyes.

Still, for all of his loving characteristics, there were signs that this Lab had suffered more than an injured head; he had suffered a wound to his heart, too.

One day, not long after he came to live here, he followed me to the garden shed where I grabbed a rake to tidy up the yard. The change in him was instantaneous. His head

drooped, his tail went between his legs, and fear shone in his eyes. He saw something in my hand and thought I was going to strike him with it. That's when I determined what most likely had happened to his head. I had suspected, but now I was sure. I dropped the rake, loved on him, and tried to reassure him that he never would be hit again.

That heartbreaking routine would repeat itself for nearly a year until Sam finally realized that he really was in a safe place. Now, I can have a yard tool or dog brush or even a hammer in my hand, and he no longer cowers.

We do have our little setbacks, however. Once, when my parents were visiting, my dad, a dog person who calls Sam a "gentle soul," grabbed a shovel to clean up some of the mess that the dogs had made in the back yard. Even though the two had been playing fetch earlier, and Sam had been following my dad around the yard for a couple days, that shovel changed everything. Sam planted himself by my side, staying where he knew it was safe, and carefully watched my dad. No way was he going anywhere near him with that "stick" in his hand. Even now, he's very leery of men with something in their hand. That speaks volumes to me.

Sam also still tends to gobble his food and treats like he has to compete for it. Or maybe, in the back of his mind, he's not sure when—or if—another meal will be forthcoming. Neither is true, of course, and we'll never stop proving that to him.

He can be a little too energetic at times, which may explain why someone whacked him. He jumps all around you—but not on you—when he's really excited to see you, but all that requires is a firm voice to make him calm down. But who could ever get angry at such joy?

Now, all that love and enthusiasm is returned to him, and he's blossomed because of it. These days, all Sam has to worry about is whether someone will play fetch with him, and, boy, they'd better be ready, because he takes it seriously. Sam reveals his Lab traits with razor-sharp intensity when we play. He stands stock still, moving only his eyes, shifting his gaze between my eyes and the ball to determine where I'm going to throw it. Usually, I'll point and say, "That way," and as I draw my arm back to throw, he's already at a dead run. His great joy is catching it on the first bounce. Mine, too, because he gets so proud of himself. If Sammy had his way, we would play fetch 24 hours a day. He'd rather play than eat.

Yes, he's full of energy, but he also has a gentle, perceptive part of his personality that makes him irresistible. That particularly came through when we brought 9-week-old Abby, a Great Pyrenees, home after losing Maggie.

Abby had to stay in the house for the first few days for fear that Sam would get a little too gregarious with her. But there was no need to worry. This big boy who knocks over grills as he chases balls, runs until his chest would explode, and leaps high up in the air just because he's happy to see you, treated Baby Abby with tenderness. He instinctively knew that she needed to be handled gently and carefully. When they played tug-of-war, he let her win. When she crawled all over him, he would lie extra still so she wouldn't tumble off. When she would chase him and bite his ear or tail, he never got angry. He might yelp in pain, but he never, ever snapped back.

Now that Abby's grown, the two are inseparable. They eat together. They sleep together. They doze in the sun together. And they patrol the yard together. If you see one, the other isn't very far away.

Friends tease me about being too indulgent of my dogs. A garden shed the size of a one-car garage has been converted to their house, complete with a framed bed of soft cedar shavings, windows, a night-light, and, in winter, a heat lamp. Sam has his own kiddie pool for the summer. They get toys and treats. And they get showered with attention.

But when you have a survivor like Sam, you want to make their life as wonderful as possible. For a dog who had such a rough experience at the hands of abusive and uncaring people, he is one of the most loving, happy, playful dogs I have ever known. His loving nature, a Labrador characteristic, overcame a trauma that easily could have turned him into a mistrustful, mean dog.

Instead, he adores his "sister," Abby, he greets every visitor—even the man who checks the electric meter—with his favorite ball just in case they might want to play, and he shows doting affection to everyone in his life. He's a happy boy. You can see it in his eyes.

I look at this happy, well-adjusted, loving dog sometimes and the idea that someone could hurt him just breaks my heart. All he wants is to love and be loved. Well, and to fetch his ball, too.

This dog came here with ribs showing, an injured head, and a wounded heart. Sure, the good food, medicine, and safe home helped Sam recover. But his own loving nature helped him overcome the hurt he'd experienced, for in this dog is the power of love, forgiveness, resiliency, and trust.

Just look in his eyes; you'll see it there.

A Man and His Dog

by

Ron Schara

Ron Schara is a storyteller, a man fascinated with tales of the

outdoors. For more than thirty years he has written about his

days afield, often with a Lab by his side, for the Minneapolis

Star Tribune. He also tells his tales to millions of television

viewers through his shows *Minnesota Bound* on the Outdoor

Life Network, *Call of the Wild* on the Outdoor Channel, and

Backroads with Ron & Raven on ESPN. Raven is the current

Lab in Ron's life, and Raven's name and likeness are nearly as

well known as the author himself.

But before Raven, Ron shared his life with another Lab,

Kyla. For many years, Kyla was Ron's companion afield (and

just about everywhere else) as he pursued game throughout

the Midwest. This is the story of Kyla, a dedicated hunter to

the end.

*a*s the days cool and the leaves begin to fall, there is something in the air that is not seen.

Most of us who hunt know when it happens, although the source remains a mystery. Maybe it's the twinge in the air. Or the changing autumn landscape. Or the fall shuffle of wild game along with an inner clock of my own species that sparks something.

As a hunter, I only feel it. Kyla, the black Lab, could smell it.

But for both of us the message was the same: It was time to go hunting.

Nothing else explains Kyla's sudden left turn out of the kennel the other day. After days, weeks and months of turning right and running to her usual "go potty" spot, Kyla charged to her left for a quick sniff at the back door of the Jeep.

She bounded back and yipped once.

I didn't have to tell her I'd loaded the Jeep with a portable crate and a shotgun. Her nose told her.

It was opening day of Minnesota's pheasant season.

It was also our eleventh October as hunting companions. As we roamed the tall CRP grass, I followed Kyla, watching her twitching tail, as usual. Her tail always said what she couldn't. It told of birds close or long gone. And at times, despite hours of fruitless hunting, her tail told of not quitting.

Kyla wore her heart on her tail. Most hunting dogs do.

In fact, it's this sense of teamwork that makes the hunter-dog bond so strong. In this fraternity, there are good hunting dogs and some not so good. We've hunted with both.

But every hunting dog is worth braggin' and boastin' about. Why? Because the team—hunter and dog—has slogged through the same marsh muck, shivered in the same cold and thirsted in the heat.

Together, hunter and dog have watched the same sunrises and shared the same sandwiches. And their hearts have been fluttered by the same gaudy ringnecks.

As a teammate, Kyla was always good company. She was, in fact, the best hunting dog that ever heeled at my side. She was all a retriever should be, with a good nose and a willingness to fetch forever. Kyla also did what most retrievers don't do: She pointed—stiff as a statue—if the bird held tight.

She also was an agreeable teammate. She knew when to be quiet in the car during long drives to pheasant country. She knew it didn't pay to whine with anticipation until the roads turned to gravel, or worse.

Kyla wasn't perfect, of course. She never came into season so she never had puppies. She knew a blast of the whistle meant "sit," but she sometimes didn't hear it. Dog trainer Tom Dokken used to say, "Kyla is a high-maintenance dog." It was a kind way of saying Kyla often forgot who was supposed to be in charge.

No, she wasn't perfect, but awfully close to it, if you don't mind a little bragging.

Last week, Kyla and I headed for South Dakota for a jaunt in what can be the utopia of bird land. On the first afternoon, west of Redfield, Kyla rousted three ringnecks and I took three shots for our three-bird limit. What a team.

It should be noted, we also were hunting slower and easier. Neither of us was as young as we used to be. At the age of 10 1/2, Kyla's muzzle had turned gray and her pace was of an elderly canine.

In the glow of our successful first-day hunt together, I silently wondered if this might be Kyla's last year as a member of the team. Even the thought of it was painful.

Last year or not, we would hunt again tomorrow.

It was late in the afternoon, hot and dry, when we joined up with friends for a walk into a vast field of CRP land near Pierre, South Dakota. Within the first 200 yards, a flock of pheasants burst into the air. Somebody dropped a ringneck, and Kyla fetched the dead bird to me.

She was panting hard from the heat. Twenty-five minutes later, Kyla's panting had turned to heavy heaving of her lungs. She refused water. Suddenly, she quit walking. We rushed Kyla to be cooled off in a farm pond. Gradually, her panting slowed, but her back legs were paralyzed. Heat stroke? Heart attack?

"It could have been both; the symptoms are classic," said Kyla's vet, Norb Epping of Coon Rapids, Minnesota.

Several hours later, Kyla seemed to be recovering. She was laying upright, her eyes watching my every move.

"You gonna be OK?" I asked.

For the answer I looked at Kyla's tail, the tail that told all. It didn't move.

Early the next morning, Kyla died.

"Kyla went the way she would have wanted to go, hunting," Epping said.

Yes, but the rest of the team is hurting.

Old Spook and the Last Duck Hunt

by

Kenny Salwey

Kenny Salwey may just be the last river rat to haunt the shores of the Mississippi River. He cut his milk teeth on a canoe paddle and seasoned it with Mississippi mud. He's a hunter, trapper, outdoor guide, self-sufficient woodsman, and storyteller whose two books, *The Last River Rat* and *Tales of a River Rat*, have become regional classics.

Born in the Mississippi River hill country of West Central Wisconsin, Salwey dreamed from childhood of becoming a river rat. And throughout his years along the Mississippi, he always had a dog at his side—usually a Lab of some sort.

In this tale from *The Last River Rat*, Salwey tells of one of his long-time friends, his Lab mix, Spook, and their last hunting trip together.

*I*t was late in the summer of my twenty-third year and I was standing with one foot up on a chunk of firewood, both elbows resting on top of a snowfence that formed a circle about twenty feet across. Inside the fence were two dogs: one a golden retriever, the other a cross-breed long-haired, black mutt. Standing alongside me was an old river man named Ottmar Probst. Ottmar wore bib overalls and chewed Copenhagen snuff. His fingers were the size of Polish sausages. Ottmar had hunted and trapped and fished for a living on the Great River all of his life. He knew about all there was to know about gill netting, seining, and set-lining for fish. He knew about turtle trapping and hooking them under the ice. He knew the ancient art of net-making and mending. He knew about pickling and smoking fish and meat of all descriptions. Ottmar was one of the great old-time river rats, and I wanted to live like him.

My attention, however, was riveted on the black dog frolicking and jumping about. He was of medium height and weight, somewhat sinewy and thin in the ribs. "What's his name?" I asked.

"Spook," Ottmar grunted.

I called to the dog, "Here, Spook. Here, Spook." The dog came over to the fence where I stood. I reached down and petted him, scratched his ears. He sat down, closing his eyes with pleasure. I opened his mouth. My Pa always said a good dog's got a black roof in his mouth. This dog did. I patted him on the head and away he went. I asked Ottmar how much he wanted for the black dog.

Looking me square in the eye, he sputtered, "You want him? You can have him for nothing. If you don't want him, I'll shoot him first thing in the morning. Got no room here for two dogs!" As if to emphasize that statement, Ottmar took a three-fingered dip of snuff and spit a long brown stream of tobacco juice into the hot summer's dust at his feet.

I loaded the dog into my battered old car. I had long since removed the back seat because I needed the extra room for hauling trap stakes, canoes, and such. With the seat gone, I could easily slide these items in through the trunk and on into the space where the back seat was once fastened. Now, the inside of my car could smell like anything from beaver, muskrats, and ducks to catnip, wild ginger, and ginseng depending on the time of year. Might even find a chub or a creek sucker stuck in a corner from a fishing trip a week or two earlier. Spook was busy looking and smelling in every nook and cranny he could find. This pleased me for it showed he was aggressive and probably had a good nose.

We drove over to my father-in-law's place. Old Bill had a spare doghouse and chain. When I let Spook out of the car, he promptly got into a hell of a fight with old Bill's police dog. Though he was much smaller, Spook showed the toughness and determination that was to become his trademark. Old Bill and I got them apart and tied Spook up at his new home. We figured Spook to be about a year old, because he would fight and lift his leg to pee, signs that he was about full-grown.

The month wore on and soon it was the tag end of September. The autumn sun felt good to Spook and me as I threw the dummy out for him to retrieve again and again. We sat under a swamp birch and rested. I rubbed his ears as we looked into each other's eyes. Over the last three weeks since I got him, we worked on and off most every day like this, working then sitting a spell, eating lunch together and most of all just getting to know one another. Spook learned to sit and stay fairly well. He also learned to get the dummy both on land and in the water, showing great enthusiasm and desire to please. By now the young dog was a nice quiet rider in the canoe.

About ten days later came the opening day of duck season. Spook and I went deep into the Whitman Swamp where we chose to hunt on the Tent Camp Slough. Where there's water, shelter from the wind, and large oaks you'll find wood ducks feeding on acorns. Spook and I found a nice, dry place to sit at the base of an ancient, gnarled white oak tree. The bank rose gently from the water to about five feet in height. We waited for noon, which was shooting time.

Shortly after noon, a beautiful drake wood duck came flying down the slough, twisting and turning, making its way between the branches of the trees that lined both banks of the slough. Its iridescent head shone brilliant in the Autumn sun. I raised my gun, started behind the flying drake, pulled up to him, saw the barrel go slightly past his head, then I pulled the trigger all in one motion. *Bang*! I saw the duck crumple. *Ka-plop*, it hit the water. I looked at Spook; every muscle was tense, every nerve quivering as he sat at the edge of the water. "Fetch!" I called sharply. He plunged hard into the water, green duckweed spraying in every direction. Quickly, he swam and lunged his way through the shallow water and sticky black mud until he reached the duck. He sniffed the bird. Swam around it once or twice. Sniffed again, then came back without it. Upon reaching the bank he shook himself off, rolled in the leaves, then turned, and looked at me as if to say, "That bird don't look or smell like something I want to carry in *my* mouth, pal!"

About that time I remembered what an old river man had once told me: "You got to know more than the dog does in order to teach him how to hunt." So, I put the gun up against a tree, walked down to the edge of the water, pulled up my rubber hip boots, and called for Spook. Together we waded through that black, boot-sucking, Mississippi mud out to where the duck lay. I opened Spook's mouth, stuck the duck in it, and held his mouth shut until we got back to the bank.

From that day on, Spook was a swamp dog. A swamp dog is a working dog. It has to fight critters. Its face is scarred. Its ears are tattered and it has to learn which critters it can tangle with and which ones it can't. A swamp dog has to know in which direction the camps are located on a black summer night with thunder crashing and lightning striking all around us. A swamp dog needs to get us home during a frigid, blinding snowstorm with January's white winter winds howling down the Great River Valley, sweeping across the open, ice-covered marshes, and leaving nothing untouched by their bitterness. After a few years of "ice walking," I will follow my dog across the thin, first ice of the season. I will trust my life to my dog, for they seem to develop a sixth sense about where the ice is safe to travel. A swamp dog has to keep on putting one foot ahead of the other, no matter how cold or hot, hungry or thirsty they are.

As the years passed, Spook and I became inseparable. Each September, we combed the hardwood forests of the hill country surrounding the Mississippi for roots and herbs. Day after autumn day we hunted ducks, squirrels, rabbits, partridges, and pheasants. In late fall and throughout winter, we trapped 'coon, 'rats, beaver, and mink. Come spring, we fished for trout in the many tributaries of the Big River and all summer long we fished the Mississippi shorelines for catfish, sheephead, bass, and other assorted finned creatures. It was just the two of us touching, smelling, hearing, seeing, tasting, and feeling nature as if each day was the last on Earth.

One day my wife asked me to bring Spook into the house at night. "He's five years old and its cold and wet outside," she chastised me. Now, I was brought up on a small, dirt-poor farm in the hill country, a short distance from the river. We were not accustomed to having our dogs in the house no matter what the weather. But by now Spook was the best friend I'd ever had in this world, human or critter, so in the house he came. From

then on Spook went wherever I did. Day and night we were together, working, playing, and living as family. Over the course of the years, we suffered the sorrows and hardships of making a living with nature as well as experienced the joys and delights.

After spending sixteen years with me in the backwaters and bluffs along the Mississippi, old Spook's face showed the scars of many swamp battles. His hind legs were withering. He walked with a limp. I could tell that as he lay by the cabin door, the autumn sun felt good to his old bones. I knelt down beside him and held his weary old head in my hands. Looking into his eyes I saw that gray, dull appearance that meant his spirit was fading. I murmured to him, "Old, Spook, it's time you and me had one last duck hunt together."

That next morning we were up before dawn. The dark air was cold and damp, but the woodfire made the old Big Lake Shack feel quite comfortable. After a hearty breakfast, we left the camp and walked down to the edge of Big Lake. As I readied the canoe, old Spook stood by the water listening to the sounds of the night critters and sniffing the air like old dogs will. I picked Spook up and set him in the bow of the canoe on an old coat. I stepped into the stern, picked up my old poling stick, and set off across the swamp. As we wound down through the slough, I remembered the thousands of times we'd passed by these same trees, islands, and beaver dams both by canoe and on the winter's ice. A half-hour later, we came to the Tent Camp Slough. We left the canoe, walking down the east bank until we came to that same big, gnarly, old swamp white oak we'd sat by sixteen years earlier. I spread out a couple of gunnysacks and laid my tattered wool hunting coat on top. Spook and I sat there waiting for daylight.

A barred owl hooted its lonesome, eerie call from across the slough, signaling the end of another night's hunt. The trees began to take shape as a misty fog rose from the water in the haunting half light of dawn. Moisture fell from the trees. As the drops hit the water in a steady *drip-drip-drip*, they reminded me of the sands of time: steady, unrelenting, slipping away.

When it was light enough to shoot, I saw several small flocks of wood ducks trading back and forth along the slough. Suddenly, a single drake came dodging and weaving its way down the slough. I shouldered the gun, followed, swung through, then slapped the trigger. *Boom!* The bird cartwheeled end over end toward the water and splashed down.

Old Spook staggered to his feet, toddled down to the water, slipped in, and made his way slowly to the duck. He picked the bird up, turned, and brought it toward the bank. I picked up my gun and made my way to the edge of the water. I stood there, silently waiting for the dog to reach the bank. When old Spook got just close enough, I set the gun against a tree, reached down, and helped him up the bank. I patted his head and said, "Good boy, Spook, good boy!" I dried him off with a gunnysack for he was too weak to roll in the leaves.

I sat down under the oak tree. The sun began to burn the fog off the water. I laid the duck by my knee. Spook turned around once or twice then curled up between my legs with his nose close to the duck at my knee. He could smell the two things he loved most in the world: The scent of duck and me.

As we sat there together I remembered the pleasant days of summer, leisurely, long, and full of life; the bitter, snow-filled days when the swamp takes on the appearance of a white desert; the days of the thawing sun, a warm breeze, a blackbird, and the promise of spring. But now it was fall, the time of harvest and death for plants and critters alike. We heard goose-talk from a high flock following their ancient southern pathways in the sky. Across the slough, a pair of gray squirrels worked in the autumn leaves gathering acorns for winter. In years past, old Spook would have treed them for sure and then looked back at me to see if I was coming to get one for supper. Not today. No, today he lay quietly resting. I placed my hand on his chest, feeling it slowly rise and fall. From across the Great River in Minneiska, Minnesota, I heard a church bell toll its lonesome song. It was Sunday morning. In my mind's eye I could see the people, all dressed up, filing past the preacher at the door. Shaking hands, then hurrying on with their lives. The diesel engines of a towboat hummed as they pushed their way upstream in the river's main channel.

How long we sat in our special place I don't know. I recall wishing I could stop the sands of time like the sun had stopped the dripping of the dew and fog from the trees. But the Circle of Life must go on, so we loaded up our canoe and headed for camp.

A few days later, old Spook was gone. He died peaceably near the front door of Big Lake shack. I buried him in a special place. There have been other swamp dogs since and we have always begun our life together by visiting old Spook's grave where we sit a spell and remember the days gone by, the time that is now, and ponder what is yet to come.

Spook taught me many lessons. He taught me the true meaning of friendship. He taught me that when you start a job, you finish it no matter what. Old Spook helped me better understand the great Circle of Life. Death and life are one and the same, for without death there would be no new life. There would be no room for new life, nothing would be returned to the Earth. In order to have life we must have death. We cannot have one without the other. Most of all, I learned that the old saying "It is better to have loved someone or something and lost them, than to have never loved at all" is most certainly true. Even though the body is gone, the spirit is in the wind, earth, fire, and water. For as long as the mists rise from the waters at dawn and the whippoorwill calls at dusk, we will be there together. One day, I'll feel a cold nose nudge my hand, I'll look down and there by my side, sniffing the wind will be a dog called old Spook.